IS MARRIAGE NECESSARY?

IS MARRIAGE NECESSARY?

Lawrence Casler, Ph.D.

HUMAN SCIENCES PRESS

A Division of Behavioral Publications, Inc.

New York

Library of Congress Catalog Number 73-18236

ISBN: 0-87705-132-1

Copyright © 1974 by Human Sciences Press, a division of Behavioral Publications, Inc., 72 Fifth Avenue, New York, New York 10011

Printed in the United States of America
456789   987654321

Library of Congress Cataloging in Publication Data

Casler, Lawrence.
    Is marriage necessary?

    Bibliography: p. 211
    1. Marriage.   I. Title.
    HQ728.C315   301.42   73-18236

Table of Contents

Preface

THE PURPOSE OF this book is to inform, remind, or persuade the reader that the institution of marriage, as we know it, need not and should not be taken for granted. The presentation is by no means a balanced one. Rather than strive for internal balance, I have attempted to redress an imbalance. The pro-marriage orientation of our society is so pervasive that little would be gained by repeating the favorable comments so abundantly available from the pulps, pulpits, and picture tubes. Most of the material in these pages is, therefore, critical—sometimes highly critical—of marriage.

Whenever possible, each observation is documented by references to relevant research. Sometimes, however, no pertinent evidence is available, thus requiring resort to more subjective forms of buttressing. In some chapters, the reader will note a rather heavy reliance on quotations. These should neither be accepted as proof, nor rejected as inconsequential. They are primarily intended to counteract other appeals to authority with which the reader may be more familiar. The path will then be cleared for independent evaluation.

If, as Edwards has put it, marriage has become a habit, a book such as this is bound to arouse some animosity. Let it be constructive animosity. We all favor those social institutions that are conducive to human happiness and growth. Has marriage contributed to our attainment of these goals, or has it taken us further away from them? If marriage has helped some people to reach these goals, does it necessarily help *all* people? Does society have the right to stigmatize non-marital relationships? Have marriage, and the family experiences to which it gives rise, so limited our imagination and our humanity that we can no longer tolerate attempts to find joy and self-respect in unconventional ways?

With more and more people seeking alternatives to traditional marital arrangements, it is more and more essential to subject both the old and the new to careful scrutiny. Marriage is not for everybody, but neither are any of the alternatives that have yet been proposed. The basic message of this book is that we should all be free to develop relationships most conducive to the growth and happiness of ourselves and our partners. But mature freedom requires rational evaluation of the various options available. The bases for such an evaluation are included in the pages that follow.

Acknowledgments

Acknowledgment is hereby gratefully made to the following publishers, organizations, and individuals who have granted permission to reprint excerpts from the indicated publications.

American Psychological Association: H. Orlansky, "Infant care and personality." *Psychological Bulletin*, 1949, *46*, 1–48.

George Allen and Unwin, Ltd.: B. Wootton, *Social science and social pathology*. London: George Allen and Unwin, 1959.

Annual Reviews, Inc.: C. Eriksen, "Personality." *Annual Review of Psychology*, 1957, *8*, 185–210.

Appleton-Century-Crofts: W. Kenkel, *The family in perspective*. New York: Appleton-Century-Crofts, 1960; and H. Otto: *The family in search of a future*. New York: Appleton-Century-Crofts, 1970.

Columbia Forum: J. Mayer, "Toward a non-Malthusian population policy." *Columbia Forum*, 1969, *12* (2), 5–13. Copyright 1969 by the Trustees of Columbia University in the City of New York.

Constable Publishers: R. de Pomerai, *Marriage, past, present and future*. London: Constable, 1930.

Harvard University Press: M. Spiro, *Kibbutz: Venture in utopia*. Cambridge: Harvard University Press, 1955.

Holt, Rinehart and Winston, Inc.: E. Groves, *Marriage.* (Rev. ed.) New York: Henry Holt, 1941.

Institute for Sex Research, Inc.: A. Kinsey, W. Pomeroy, C. Martin, and P. Gebhard, *Sexual behavior in the human female.* Philadelphia: Saunders, 1953.

International Universities Press, Inc.: J. Tanner and B. Inhelder (Eds.), *Discussions on child development.* Vol. 2. New York: International Universities Press, 1954.

Journal Press: M. Geber, "The psycho-motor development of African children in the first year, and the influence of maternal behavior." *Journal of Social Psychology,* 1958, *47*, 185–195.

Liveright Publishing Corporation: R. Lowie, *Primitive society.* New York: Boni and Liveright, 1920.

Macmillan Publishing Co., Inc.: R. Briffault, *The mothers.* New York: Macmillan, 1927.

Macmillan Services Limited: E. Westermarck, *A short history of marriage.* London: Macmillan, 1926.

McGraw-Hill Book Co.: R. Baber, *Marriage and the family.* (Rev. ed.) New York: McGraw-Hill, 1953.

William Morrow and Co., Inc.: M. Mead, *Coming of age in Samoa.* In *From the South Seas.* New York: William Morrow, 1939.

National Psychological Association for Psychoanalysis, and R. Spitz. R. Spitz, "Diacritic and coenesthetic organization." *Psychoanalytic Review,* 1945, *32*, 146–162.

North Holland Publishing Co., and N. O'Connor. N. O'Connor, "The evidence for the permanently disturbing effects of mother-child separation."*Acta Psychologica,* 1956,*12*, 174–191.

W. W. Norton and Co., Inc. O. English and G. Pearson, *Emotional problems of living.* (Rev. ed.) New York: Norton, 1955.

Random House, Inc./Alfred A. Knopf, Inc. S. de Beauvoir, *The second sex.* Translated by H. Parshley. New York: Bantam Books, 1961. Copyright held by Alfred A. Knopf, Inc.

Random House, Inc./Alfred A. Knopf, Inc.: A. de Tocqueville, *Democracy in America.* Translated by H. Reeve. (Rev. ed.) New York: Knopf, 1945.

Porter Sargent Publisher: R. Briffault and B. Malinowski, *Marriage: Past and present.* Boston: Porter Sargent, 1956.

Texas Reports on Biology and Medicine: M. Ashley Montagu, "The sensory influences of the skin." *Texas Reports on Biology and Medicine*, 1953, *11*, 291–301.

University of Colorado Law Review. H. Hefner, "The legal enforcement of morality." *University of Colorado Law Review*, 1968, *40*, 199–221.

I

The Origins of Marriage

LIKE LANGUAGE, CRIME, AND CLOTHING, marriage has been a part of human experience for so long that attempts to understand its origins seem doomed to the limbo of unprovable speculation. There is, in fact, the danger that too great a concentration on marriage's past history may blind us to questions of current functioning and future prospects. Statements such as, "If it's been going on for so long it must be good" serve no constructive purpose; let us recall that "the wisdom of the ages" has at various times claimed that the earth is flat, that rocket flights to the moon are impossible, etc. So while we may be respectful of the past, and willing to learn from it, we should not permit ourselves to be governed by it.

Thinking about the prehistoric and historic roots of marriage may be a necessary first step toward understanding the social and psychological processes and dynamisms involved, by affording us the perspective that only history can provide, and the basis on which to consider how well marriage and the family are satisfying the needs and desires of living human beings.

2 IS MARRIAGE NECESSARY?

Evolutionary Theories

Of the many attempts to offer some sort of explanation of how marriage began, a number may be loosely characterized as evolutionary theories. These diverse theories, gaining impetus in the late nineteenth century from Darwin's exciting accounts of biological evolution, converge in proposing that the institution of marriage has followed a clear sequence, arising from certain crude animal beginnings, passing through a primitive human stage, and finally reaching its ultimate expression in the Western European ideal of the monogamous lifelong union of the male and female. More specifically, the proponents of this viewpoint suggest that the evolution began with sexual promiscuity, was followed—perhaps through some form of the "survival of the fittest" mechanism—by group marriage (a number of males sharing a number of females), proceeded to a period of polygamy (one woman with two or more husbands—polyandry—or one man with two or more wives—polygyny) and culminated in the present one/to/one marriage pattern.

There is a surface plausibility to this. The promiscuity of many animals is well known, as are the decidedly unmonogamous customs of certain so-called primitive societies. But even though the theory may offer a certain sense of orderly development and direction,[1] it is accepted by very few contemporary scholars.

One reason for rejecting the theory is that many types of mating patterns—"free love," "polygamy" and "monogamy"—can be found in the animal kingdom, with no apparent correlation with evolutionary status. Thus, some birds form monogamistic attachments, while other species are polygamous or promiscuous.[2] Similar-

[1]All superscripts refer to footnotes which can be found in the Notes section beginning on p. 185.

ly, some primates seem to practice monogamy while others, equally high on the evolutionary scale, do not; as Scott pointed out in 1968,* the gibbon is "the only one of the apes which shows anything like the human nuclear family." This absence of confirmation at the infra-human level does not automatically invalidate the evolutionary theory, but it does make us less confident in it than we might otherwise be, and it did prompt Scott to suggest, in 1962, that "anthropologists re-examine their evidence for the universality of the nuclear family in all human societies."

A second consideration constitutes a more serious challenge to the theory: polygamy has existed in a number of highly advanced human societies. Lowie even maintained that monogamy occurs chiefly in relatively simple societies, and that "under more complex conditions" it is found primarily among the lower classes.[3] It has also been pointed out, in opposition to the "promiscuous origins" theory, that some of the most primitive of known societies have prohibitions against premarital intercourse.[4] (This objection involves the dubious assumption that such contemporary groups as the Veddas are as "primitive" as our prehistoric progenitors—an unproved assumption, when we note that anthropologists have not yet been successful in categorizing contemporary societies according to evolutionary level.)

One version of the evolutionary position deserves particular mention, because of the considerable influence it once exerted over cultural anthropologists. Robert Briffault's *The Mothers,* published in 1927, is a massive, lavishly documented presentation of the point of view

*All relevant source and reference information will be found in the bibliography at the end of the book. Numbers in brackets after bibliographic entries refer to the original source pages from which direct quotes were taken.

that an original state of promiscuity was followed (perhaps after an interim of group marriage) by a woman-dominated social organization that finally gave way to the patriarchal system prevalent in the Western world today. However, another well-known student of the subject, Bronislaw Malinowski, has presented ethnographic evidence in the *Encyclopaedia Britannica* indicating that the theory is "based on an inadequate analysis of the institution [of marriage] and an unwarranted assumption of early sexual and economic communism as well as group motherhood."

On the other hand, some support for the evolutionary theory—but not necessarily of the Briffault variety—stems from the finding that women (and other female mammals) that mate promiscuously tend to have fewer offspring than those with single mates. From this it follows that monogamy and polygyny would be, in the long run, more successful than polyandry in terms of biological perpetuation. This expectation is confirmed by the fact that polyandry is currently found in far fewer societies than either monogamy or polygyny.

Nevertheless, the approach does not adequately explain the numerous varieties of marital patterns that co-exist today. To claim that monogamy developed out of polygamy is just as arbitrary as claiming the reverse. This is not to say that the evolutionary approach is "wrong," but only that it is incomplete. By confining itself to questions of *how* marriage has developed, it neglects the even more basic question of *why* marriage developed. For this latter purpose, an alternative orientation is necessary.

The Functionalist Approach

Men and women existed before there was marriage. The various types of marriage have emerged, we may assume, in response to the individual and collective needs of human beings. The functionalist approach attempts to uncover the original functions of marriage.[5] This approach, like the evolutionary approach, is necessarily speculative, but while we can only guess at the initial psychological and social functions of marriage, the combination of behavioral science and common sense may help us to guess wisely.

Sex. Was the first function of marriage to provide a regular source of sexual gratification? Briffault has stated in *The Mothers*, "The institution, its origin and development, have been almost exclusively viewed and discussed by social historians in terms of the operation of the sexual instincts and of the sentiments connected with those instincts." In fact, sexuality has even been invoked to explain the origins of the particular type of matrimony currently favored in the Western world. Thorpe has asserted that the almost constant sexual receptivity of human females (as contrasted with the periodic receptivity typical of other species) renders polygamy unnecessary. "Monogamy," he concludes, "is the natural state of man." But Thorpe fails to explain why monogamy would be preferred over other options, nor does he convincingly account for the fact that marriage generally occurs even in those societies that are quite permissive about pre-marital intercourse. His theory is further weakened by the fact that, since many of these societies have sanctions against adultery, marriage may reduce, rather than increase, the opportunities for satisfying the sex drive. (The extent to which this statement is valid in contemporary Western civilization will be examined in detail later.)

Despite the foregoing considerations, it would probably be erroneous to suppose that sexual attraction played *no* role in the initiation of marriage-like relationships. An individual who has enjoyed the charms of a particular sexual partner may learn to associate this mate with the idea of sexual satisfaction and may, therefore, seek to make the relationship permanent. But is it not equally possible that the learned association is between sexual pleasure and females (or males) in general, rather than particular individuals? If so, then promiscuous mating would be a likely consequence.

Closely related to the individual function of sexual gratification is the social function of sexual organization or regulation. Many sociologists, including Davis, have suggested that complete sexual freedom would result in anarchy and social disintegration. No evidence exists on this point, however, and the most that can be said with any confidence is that significant social changes (new patterns of housing, alterations in inheritance laws, reductions in parental control, etc.) would probably result. But social change is not synonymous with social disintegration.

The one form of sexual regulation that *may* be essential for societal survival is the incest taboo.[6] While convincing explanation of the near universality of incest taboos is still not available,[7] it appears likely that the husband's proprietary rights over his wife would be especially jealously protected against the son's potential encroachments. And, as has just been proposed, such a competitive situation can best be understood in terms of a pre-existing marital relationship.

The question of social control of sexual behavior is exceedingly complex. Although such control may have contributed to the inception of marriage, it seems reasonable to assume that marriage would not have arisen unless other factors were also involved.

Economic Factors. We know that our earliest ancestors, long before the development of farming and animal husbandry, were food-gatherers. Whether the environment primarily offered edible plants or edible animals, our forebears would have had to travel farther and farther from home or to build a succession of temporary shelters. Man must quite early have realized that for defense against human or animal poachers, as well as for maintenance, it would be well to have someone watch his home site (and keep the indispensable home fire burning) while he was out working. Perhaps a trial-and-error period ensued, the upshot of which was that females—who were not particularly good food-gatherers because of their subjection to the frequent incapacities associated with reproduction—would be well suited for the job of staying home. Likewise, they were the logical choices for such domestic chores as clothes-making and cooking. The sexual division of labor had begun. Both parties benefited: the males had more time each day in which to gain livelihoods and the females were assured of provisions even during the less active periods of their lives. In some of the more primitive contemporary societies, this economic function is still very much in evidence. Thus, Lowie stated in 1920 that "a Kai does not marry because of desires he can readily gratify outside of wedlock without assuming any responsibilities; he marries because he needs a woman to make pots and to cook his meals, to manufacture nets and weed his plantation, in return for which he provides the household with game and fish and builds the dwelling." Westermarck commented similarly, in 1926, that "a woman on the Congo is the best gilt-edged security in which a man can invest his surplus wealth."

At least a part of this "gilt edge" probably stemmed from the recognition that women would produce offspring who would make their own contributions to the domestic economy. (Indeed, these considerations predominated even in such an exalted culture as the

Greek; as Demosthenes said, "Mistresses we keep for the sake of pleasure, concubines for the daily care of our persons, but wives to bear us legitimate children and to be faithful guardians of our household.")

Given the above, a change in economic conditions might be expected to drastically change a society's attitude toward marriage. In Uganda, as Briffault pointed out in 1927, when such a change occurred, the men "no longer [depended] on household production and on the cultivation of the fields by the women....The economic motive for individual marriage having disappeared, there is no other left; they therefore no longer desire to marry."

Briffault was led to conclude that "the origin, like the biological foundation, of individual marriage [is] essentially economic....In the vast majority of uncultured societies marriage is regarded almost exclusively in the light of economic considerations, and throughout by far the greater part of the history of the institution the various changes which it has undergone have been conditioned by economic causes."

Briffault has elsewhere claimed, in the book he wrote with Malinowski, not only that marriage itself is a product of economic conditions, but also that our particular monogamistic form of the institution is explicable in economic terms. His tracing of monogamy back to the agricultural economy of ancient Greece is not always clear or persuasive, but it does represent an admirable attempt to revivify the evolutionist point of view within a more rational framework. Church has proposed a variant of this theory: "Marriage is proprietary. It arose when the caveman, swayed by a strong taste for ownership, beat woman, hampered by recurrent pregnancies, into chattelship. When progress improved woman's lot, she, as proud wife or fiancée, caught the idea of making her owner a chattel."

But this economic interpretation is not enough. The fact that, as Malinowski pointed out in 1960, "economic obligations ... cutting across the closed unity of the household could be quoted from every single tribe of which we have adequate information," suggests that economic needs were not entirely dependent upon marriage, so that this function, as an explanatory principle, must be augmented or supplemented by others. One attempt at augmentation has been offered by the anthropologist Edward Tylor, who proposed that matrimony was preponderantly a means of cementing group alliances between families or clans. There is some evidence to support this view, but families existed before alliances between them could take place, and Tylor's theory does not shed light on the ultimate origins of these. The theory, however, can be taken one step further. Let us suppose that a group of people existed in some prehistoric, pre-marital epoch, and that the most pressing need of the group was for sheer physical survival. Let us suppose, further, that the group encountered another group, likewise free of marriage and likewise intent on survival. Competition for food and shelter might soon ensue, and the mutual distrust and hostility would make such demands on the time and energy of both groups that their chances of survival would progressively decrease. This crisis could result in a decision to join forces. The social union might well include an exchange of women, and as long as some of the women from each group were living amid the other group, the intergroup ties would remain secure. The women would become, in essence, hostages. Marriage, if this line of thinking is correct, was thus a social invention, necessitated by basic survival needs. The incest taboo arose in order to assure that the members of each subsequent generation would be available as partners (hostages) to members of the other group.

It is readily acknowledged that these speculations beg a number of questions and raise a number of others. They are intended, merely, to suggest a possible extension of Tylor's theory. But insistence on the economic function, no matter how extended, obscures what is, to many students of the subject, the primary function of marriage.

Child Rearing. Malinowski, after his 1960 cross-cultural survey of marriage customs, regulations governing divorce, etc., concludes that "the institution of marriage is primarily determined by the needs of the offspring, by the dependence of the children upon their parents." This function is a particularly apparent part of our Judeo-Christian heritage; as Kenkel has pointed out, "The Hebrew woman's role as a mother undoubtedly received a greater emphasis than any of her other roles." And this tradition is itself a reflection of still earlier influences. Sir Leonard Woolley makes the point that in ancient Sumer, the source of many Hebrew traditions, the wife's "position in the house was rendered precarious by the imperious demand of the peoples of the Near East for children to carry on the name; barrenness, if it did not dissolve the marriage tie, at least deprived the wife of her exclusive rights of wedlock." He goes on to say, "In marriage the personality of the wife was subordinate to her function as mother: if childlessness were due not to physical inabilities but to the wife's refusal of conjugal relations, she was thrown into the water and drowned." So, too, as Lowie wrote in 1933, among the African Longo (and many other African societies), "barrenness exposed a wife to contempt and divorce."

This emphasis on marriage for procreation is scarcely surprising. The fundamental goal, *sine qua non*, of a society is to keep itself going. Although reproduction is not the only means of social perpetuation, it is generally more reliable and more manageable than recruiting from other societies. Furthermore, the family is usually the primary medium through which cultural patterns are transmitted to the new generation.[8] But we must not fall into the trap of concluding that culture-transmission is necessarily *dependent* upon the family. There are some societies in which the children are brought up in non-familial group settings. We will probably never know why these societies did not adopt the more usual child-rearing arrangements, but their very existence is enough to disprove any claims that familial upbringing is either universal or necessary.

Despite the considerable social importance of child-production, one must disagree with Malinowski when he claims, in his debate with Briffault, that "a man in any country or at any level of culture marries when he wants children; or, more truly, perhaps, marries when his sweetheart desires to have children." This seems to be another instance of placing the cart before the horse. There were certainly children in the world before there were marriages, and the idea that children were desirable only when they were born in wedlock must have arisen *after* the development of wedlock.

Perhaps a more basic explanation for the close connection between child-rearing and primitive marriage can be deduced from the the fact that a suckling infant gives the mother immediate gratification by relieving the uncomfortable pressure of milk in the breasts (see page 71). The mother would, then, become attached to the baby (this attachment being, perhaps, the forerunner of what we call "mother love"); and the father—or, at any rate, the mother's current mate—would have to maintain the baby in order to keep the woman. Furthermore, the rigors of child-bearing and rearing would render the mother increasingly dependent on the mate who supplies the food, erects the shelter, etc. The economic determinants discussed earlier may therefore have been strongly reinforced by the exigencies of biology, with the woman agreeing to perform domestic tasks and to take care of the valued offspring, on the condition that the man agrees to be the provider of material necessities. Such bargains, at first largely dependent on mutual trust, may well have been eventually supplanted by more binding contractual agreements, witnessed and recognized by members of the community. And thus would formal marriage have begun.

There are other aspects of propagation that may have been very important to our forebears. There was, for example, the matter of economic security: when parents grew too old to work, their children may have been expected to support them. Also, many societies have had beliefs about the after-life that require the rendering of prayers or sacrifices by the surviving offspring.

Legitimacy. One of the functions most often proposed by sociologically oriented commentators has to do with conferring status upon offspring. The emphasis on legitimacy may have resulted, in some cases, from the desire to transmit wealth along blood lines, or to solidify intergroup alliances. But other factors were probably also involved. As Ashley Montagu has put it, in his contribution to the Briffault-Malinowski volume, "In a good many societies a child cannot be fitted into the structure of society if the clan and moiety membership of the father is not known. Hence an 'illegitimate' child poses an insoluble problem to such societies, so that a 'father' must be found for the child or it must be disposed of." However, despite legitimacy's very real significance in many societies, it seems to be a derivative of marriage and not an originally causal factor. The mere existence of the concept of "legitimacy" presupposes some kind of family organization. Also, as Westermarck pointed out in 1926, there are a great many cultures in which "illegitimate children are treated exactly like legitimate ones with regard to descent, inheritance, and succession." (There are, of course, a number of societies in which this function does constitute a strong inducement to marry. In some of Israel's communal settlements, for example, Talmon-Garber has reported that people marry for the sole purpose of legitimizing children. Nor is marriage for the purpose of giving a "name" to one's unborn child unfamiliar in our own society. In this connection, Bertrand Russell made a point in 1929 that will be expanded upon later: "Love as a relation between men and women was ruined by the desire to make sure of the legitimacy of children. And not only love, but the whole contribution that women can make to civilization, has been stunted for the same reason.")

Love. We come now to what, in our society, is sometimes alleged to be *the* indispensable function of marriage: the bringing together of two people in love. Some writers on the subject apparently find themselves unable to separate the ideas of love and marriage. Thus, Ludlow states that "love may be defined as that passionate and ever-present desire for two individuals to create for each other conditions which will develop their selves *more fully than if they had never been married.*"[9] Although many may reject this bald assumption that only people who are married can experience love, they may remain convinced that love and marriage are—or should be—as inextricably linked as the famed horse and carriage. It should be obvious, however, that inextricability is a temporary condition; the horse and carriage no longer go together.

Courtly love, from which romantic love probably descends, was distinctly separate from courtly marriage. As Montaigne put it, "love and marriage are two intentions that go by separate roads."[10] The custom of marrying for love is far from universal. In fact, it has long been argued that love and marriage may be antithetical, because the former must be "freely given."[11] Even in those primitive societies in which conjugal love has been observed, the temporal sequence seems frequently obscured. More often than not, as Briffault stated in *Marriage: Past and Present*, "love among savages is the result, rather than the cause of marriage." Linton has commented that the rarity of "violent attachments between persons of opposite sex. . .in most societies suggests that they are psychological abnormalities to which our own culture has attached an extraordinary value." A clue to the meaning of this Western deviation may be found in the report that those societies in which husband and wife are economically dependent upon one another have much less emphasis on conjugal love than we do. Marriages apparently require some kind of glue. Coppinger & Rosenblatt put it that, if the partners do not need each other for subsistence, the society provides the substitute mucilage of love. We may conclude, tentatively, that love—whatever its individual functions may be—is generally of only secondary sociological significance. It becomes an exalted part of a culture to the extent that the institution of marriage has no other means of support (see Goode's comments in his 1959 article).

Thus, love seems to be still another of those factors

that are considerably more significant for contemporary Western societies than for societies in other times and places. A fuller discussion of love will therefore appear in the next chapter, when the current functions of marriage are explored.

Jealousy. Despite occasional claims that jealousy is a part of "human nature," its absence from so many societies suggests that it is a culturally conditioned response. For reasons that will be made clear later (see p. 36), jealousy should probably be regarded as a result, rather than a cause, of marriage. It should not be surprising, therefore, that in those societies in which pre-marital intercourse is taken for granted, jealousy is virtually non-existent—until marriage takes place. The theory that marriage originated as a jealous attempt to eliminate rival suitors seems little more than a projection of contemporary insecurities.

Religion. Similarly, it is doubtful that marriage originally had a religious function. Religion has not always been the buttress of marriage that it is today. To quote the ubiquitous Mr. Briffault, in *The Mothers*, once again, "Marriage. . .is not regarded by peoples in lower stages of culture as in any way partaking of the character of a religious institution or ceremony."[12] He further develops this point in his 1931 article, "Free Love": "The religious grounds which bulk so large at the present day. . .are of very recent cultural origin and have in reality done little more than lend the weighty support of religious and moral sanctions to social regulations already established by economic factors."

Many religions have placed considerable emphasis on the value of matrimony, but in every case this support seems based on one or more of the other, essentially

non-religious, functions that have already been discussed: the regulation of sexual behavior, the functions
of child-bearing and child-rearing, etc. The greater the
number of offspring, and the closer the familial ties, the
more likely it is that the particular religion will increase
in number of adherents (see page 45). It is interesting
to note that the negative attitude of early Christianity
toward marriage may have been based, to a considerable
extent, on the conviction that the end of the world was
so near at hand (recall St. Paul's warning, "The time
is short") that further procreation was unnecessary.

"Instinct". There are some who believe that marriage
is simply a matter of human nature—that there is an
"instinct" to marry. This view holds that no other function of marriage is basic; instead, we marry for the obvious reason that the instinctive need must—at least for
normal men and women—be satisfied. The nature of
instinct has been a subject of discussion and dispute
among psychologists, and others, for decades. While
some students have concluded that there is no such
thing as instinct, a few authorities remain strongly convinced that nearly everything we do has an instinctive
basis. Still others have taken a compromise position—
instincts exist, but their influence on human behavior
is a limited one. The one sure proof that matrimony
is instinctive—the isolation of the specific gene or genes
responsible for marriage—is unavailable. On the other
hand, the one sure proof for the anti-instinct position—
conclusive evidence that marriage is entirely environmental in origin—is likewise beyond our present ability
to establish.

The social psychologist Otto Klineberg has suggested,
in an effort to alleviate the "instinct" problem, that the
following three criteria be applied in any case where in-

stinct is hypothesized: first, the behavior should reveal continuity with the behavior of infra-human animals; second, the behavior should have an organic basis, i.e., it should be closely related to the biochemical or physiological functioning of the organism; and third, the behavior should be found in all of the world's societies. The greater the extent to which these criteria are met, the more justifiably can the behavior be called instinctive.

The first criterion is probably least significant, being contradicted by an opposing viewpoint that asserts that behavior is most likely to be instinctive if it is "species-specific" (i.e., peculiar to a single species). Therefore, only brief use will be made of this criterion. Perhaps it will suffice to remind the reader (see pages 2-3), that the continuity with lower animals is by no means complete.

As concerns the second criterion, no organic or physiological basis for marriage is known to exist. There are, of course, physiological components of the sexual aspect of marriage; but marriage itself cannot be regarded as having a physiological basis in the same sense that salivation and pupillary dilation is organically based.

As for the third criterion, a few societies have come to light that seem to be free of marriage—at least in any form recognizable to us. These groups include the Kuni, the Aranda, Senegambians, Society Islanders, the Fuegians, and the native inhabitants of Setie and Peland.[13] According to Kenkel's survey of the anthropological literature, "Places are cited and travelers are noted who observed the near or complete absence of marriage. It has been reported, for example, that it is difficult in some societies to tell whether there is such a thing as marriage or whether the people merely practice a variation of nocturnal visiting. In other places the sexual unions are described as too transitory to warrant the term marriage." Also, Westermarck discusses, in his 1926 book, some Sumatran and Indian groups in which it was said to be customary for "the husband not to live with his wife at all, but merely to pay her visits in the place where she dwells with her maternal relatives; and the children she bears then remain with her."

The Nayar of Malabar constitutes an especially interesting example of a virtually marriage-free society. According to Westermarck's detailed account of the traditions of this group, every Nayar girl, before attaining puberty, did go through a marriage ceremony, but the husband "after receiving the customary fee," would depart and held no conjugal rights over the girl. "Subsequently she was allowed to cohabit with any Brahman or Nayar she chose, and usually she had several lovers who cohabited with her by agreement among themselves. All the lovers contributed to maintain the woman, but she lived apart from them. I call them lovers rather than husbands; for the polyandrous unions of the Nayars can hardly be called marriage even from a non-legal point of view."[14] The objection may be made that the existence of the "marriage ceremony" signifies that marriage does, in fact, exist among the Nayars. But this seems to be only a semantic quibble. The point is that the sort of relationship that we designate as marital does not exist.

While the number of societies that seem to be without marriage is relatively small, these societies do serve to seriously challenge the oft-expressed sentiment that marriage is an indispensable social institution. As Briffault said in 1927, "It would appear that the group or association which was at one time supposed to be the original unit of human society is somewhat elusive in its more primitive states. . . not only does it not exist as a psychological, juridic, or social unit; it frequently does not exist as a physical association."[15]

We have seen that none of Klineberg's three criteria is fully satisfied. According to Foote, in his *Encyclopædia Britannica* article on the family, "there is no instinctual basis universally compelling human beings to form families or to rear their young." And this conclusion is by no means recent. Briffault states in the 1927 work that, "The Roman legists never regarded marriage in the form which they themselves contributed so largely to establish as anything else than an institution, and never attempted to represent it as an inborn instinct."

The statement that *monogamy* is instinctive is, notwithstanding the justification offered by Thorpe (see page 5), even more questionable than similar statements about marriage in general. Murdock stated, in 1949, that only 43 of the 238 societies he surveyed could be classified as monogamous, when preferential marriage form was used as the criterion.[16] As Kinsey and his associates have pointed out, in *Sexual Behavior in the Human Male*, "The human male would be promiscuous . . . throughout the whole of his life if there were no social restrictions."

Even the familiar jingle, "Higamus, hogamus, woman's monogamous; Hogamus, higamus, man is polygamous," appears to lack validity. As one legal authority, G. A. Bartlett, has put it, "The important trend we see in the divorce court and even out of it is the revelation that women are little, if any, more monogamous than men."[17] Thus the assertion by an early churchman that polygamy is "contrary to the nature of man and woman" (quoted by Briffault in *The Mothers*), while typical of the narrow arrogance displayed by many commentators both before and since, cannot be taken seriously.

Although the "marriage instinct" seems untenable, the possibility remains that there *is* an instinctive tendency to establish an intimate one-to-one relationship with another human being. The need is undoubtedly a strong one in some people, but application of the Klineberg criteria clearly reveals that any attribution of instinctive status would be very tenuous indeed. The desire to "couple" may *feel* instinctive to those individuals who have strong drives in this direction, but it is doubtful that anything more is involved than the combination of a sex drive, a vulnerability to social pressures, and a learned desire for interpersonal closeness. Moreover, regardless of the instinctive nature of this drive, it should be clear that the drive can be satisfied in the absence of marriage.

A similar conclusion emerges with respect to the claim that human beings instinctively need to feel a sense of rootedness or belongingness. Such a need is present in many people, but there is no reason to assume that it can be found in everyone. The need, powerful though it may sometimes be, can probably be traced back to early family experiences, rather than to inalterable human nature. And the need can be satisfied without recourse to matrimony. Indeed, like many of the other motives we have been considering, this one seems to be more an effect than a cause of marriage.

Having rejected the instinct explanation, we are still left with the other possible marital functions discussed above. The most reasonable explanation is probably a combinative one; a multi-function theory that can take either of two forms: first, there may have been a set of universal social and/or individual needs that provided the initial instigation for marriage. (To this writer, our ancestors' economic and sexual requirements appear to be particularly likely instigators, with the function of child-rearing becoming influential very soon thereafter.[18] From this perspective, specific marital forms may have developed as institutionalized reactions to local conditions that stood in the way of the fulfillment of these primary functions. For example, in a society whose population of young men ·was periodically decimated by war, social insistence on monogamy would have caused many women to be husbandless. Polygyny would take care of this problem nicely—so nicely, in fact, that polygyny might come to be regarded in such societies as the only "natural" form of marital relationship.

Alternatively, the multi-function theory could postulate that different social groups had different needs (or sets of needs) that were not being reliably satisfied by existing social arrangements, resulting in the emergence of a new pattern of interaction that *would* satisfy these needs. Thus, some form of marriage may have arisen in one society in response to economic requirements of the group or its members, whereas the same form, or a different form, of marriage arose in another society to satisfy the requirement of regularized sexual activity, ancestor worship, and/or any of the other functions that we have been examining. Whether these speculations represent any improvement over the other speculations that have been described remains to be determined.

This chapter has presented the position that marriage is best understood as a means of satisfying specific human needs. When these needs no longer exist, or when they can be more efficiently satisfied outside of marriage, or when the needs themselves should be modified because they interfere with the full development of the individual and of the society, then marriage becomes not only unnecessary but undesirable.[19]

It is not unusual for the character of an institution

to change from beneficial to harmful, or from essential to obsolete. What *is* unusual is for such shifts to be recognized and dealt with effectively. The remainder of this book is intended to assess the value of contemporary marriage and to examine the possibility of other forms of male-female relationships.

II

Contemporary Marriage

THE MATERIAL PRESENTED in Chapter I indicates that marriage probably served, at one time, functions that made it desirable and/or necessary. We would be risking serious error, however, to conclude that marriage is *therefore* desirable and/or necessary today. Some of the original functions may have become obsolete or may have dramatically changed during the course of generations; or the functions may still exist, but more efficient means of fulfilling them may have evolved.

Because of the extensive changes between now and an earlier day in nearly every aspect of life—widespread industrialization, reliable contraceptives, increased lifespans, compulsory education, changes in residential patterns, etc.—we should not be surprised to find that marriage appears to be losing its grip. Has the institution truly outlived its usefulness, or have new functions emerged that justify its continued existence? A functional analysis will help us place contemporary marriage in proper perspective.

The functions of contemporary marriage can be loosely divided into the personal and the social. But these are nearly always so intertwined that it is neither possible nor desirable to separate them. So, at this point, we will not even try, and will simply focus our discussion on the question of why people marry. While this approach may appear at first to emphasize the individual, rather than the social, functions of marriage, it will soon be clear that the various reasons for marrying can be understood fully only if their individual *and* social foundations are made explicit.

It should be noted at the outset that primary consideration will be given to marriage in the United States; references to marriage in other societies will be made chiefly for purposes of illustration and comparison.

Sexual Functions

Is the desire for sexual gratification still a basis for marriage? Assuredly, sexual relations do play an important and sometimes focal role in marriage. But many recent surveys leave little doubt that sexual activity outside of marriage, whether pre- or extra-marital, is quite widespread. Although anyone citing the findings of Kinsey and his associates[1] must take into account the statistical and other flaws almost inevitable when such a delicate topic is searchingly explored,[2] these findings still remain the most extensive and the most reliable set of data currently available: of all the females in Kinsey's sample, nearly half had engaged in sexual intercourse outside of marriage.[3] More than a quarter of the married women who were interviewed admitted to at least one act of adultery. (The corresponding percentages for American males were 75% and 50%.)

It is striking that the frequency Murdock reported in 1950 of pre-marital intercourse among the "promiscuous" post-adolescents on the island of Truk is no greater than that revealed for most segments of our own society. The major difference seems to be that the fortunate natives of Truk were not bothered by feelings of guilt and shame—at least not until the missionaries began to exert their "civilizing" influence.[4] The United States is not alone in this pattern of widespread non-marital sexual behavior. For example, Gray's careful study involving more than 20,000 women in England and Wales who had given birth to their first child revealed that fully 80% had engaged in pre-marital intercourse. Goode reported, in 1960, that illegitimate births constitute about half of all live births in the countries of the Caribbean. And outside of the Western world, Murdock stated in 1949 that fewer than 5% of the societies that have been studied prohibit all non-marital sexual relations.

However, data such as these cannot be properly interpreted without reference to the broader considerations of social climate, economic conditions, etc. It is interesting to note, for example, Christensen's report that a particularly liberal contemporary society—Denmark—has more premarital pregnancy, but fewer "negative effects therefrom [i.e., divorce]" than the American sub-societies with which it was compared.

Clearly, while the marital relationship may be a convenient locus for sexual activity, it is by no means the only locus available. (And the point will be made, later, that it is perhaps not the *best* locus available, in terms of sheer physical gratification.) Marriage for the primary purpose of ensuring a regular source of sexual satisfaction is undertaken only by the minority for whom—because of religious or moral scruples, lack of self-confidence, or ignorance about contraceptives and prophylactics—non-marital sex is unacceptable. Furthermore, it should be obvious that the orthodoxly religious will not (consciously) enter upon marriage in order to taste the carnal fruits thereof, for precisely the same rea--·

son that non-marital sex is not open to them: sexual activity, for its own sake, is regarded as sinful.

There are, nonetheless, a sizable number of individuals who do marry chiefly out of sexual attraction and with the prospect of sexual pleasure. For any of several possible reasons (including the ancient female ploy of "this is as far as you can go until we get married"), some people are prevented from satisfying their urges in the single state, and so they marry. As to whether sexual attraction is a good reason for getting married, clergymen, psychologists, marriage counselors, divorced couples, and couples still unhappily married agree on a virtually unanimous "No!" When the honeymoon is over— and it may end the morning after the wedding night— the physical charms of one's mate may become somewhat less compelling, and the other, less glamorous aspects of married life may begin to loom large and threatening. "I see no marriages," wrote Montaigne, "which sooner fail than those contracted on account of beauty and amorous desire."[5] Somewhat more graphic is Havelock Ellis' observation that "the vagina has not always proved a very firm center for the support of marriage."

We must, of course, respect the position of those who refrain from non-marital sex on moral grounds; but all too often, "morality" is a cover-up for fear. Many young unmarrieds retain their virginity because of the triple threat of infection, detection, and conception, or the fear of frying in hell. Others may be afraid to reveal a lack of sexual skill or effectiveness. These frightened people have every right to shun sex, but the word "moral" does not seem to apply to their motives. Nor is it very convincing to maintain that pre-marital sex is immoral because immorality *means* pre-marital sex. Not only is the statement circular, but also it obscures the more meaningful understanding of morality in terms of respecting the rights of others.

There are a few exceptions to the general agreement concerning the inadvisability of marrying for sex. Consider, for example, the following pronouncement made by Clarke, as quoted in de Lys: "Let us not condemn youth either to sexual starvation or sexual promiscuousness. Let us help them attain the highest standards of sexual morality and physical and mental well-being through carefully considered early marriages." Such a proposal, however, despite its lofty language, is downright immoral. To think of one's spouse as little more than a genital with legs is as dehumanizing as it is unrealistic. In the words of Simone de Beauvoir, "Marriage is obscene in principle in so far as it transforms into rights and duties those mutual relations which should be founded on a spontaneous urge."

Another argument against the primary use of marriage as a sop to passion is Westermarck's statement in 1926 that there may be something intrinsic in the sex drive that operates *against* marriage, or at least against monogamy:

> Sexual desire is dulled by long companionship and excited by novelty....The statistics on divorce and remarriage in Europe show that the taste for variety is often the chief cause of the dissolution of marriage; and I believe it is a matter of ordinary experience that in countries where divorce is of common occurrence, sexual indifference and a desire for new gratifications of the sexual instinct are potent causes of it.

Kinsey has presented evidence that beyond the age of 40, single males may actually exceed married males in total amount of sexual activity.[6] To quote de Beauvoir again, "It is pure absurdity to maintain that two married persons . . . will provide each other with sex satisfaction as long as they live." In short, holy monogamy gives way to holy monotony.

This section of the discussion may, therefore, be summarized as follows: (a) most people do not need marriage in order to satisfy their sexual urges; (b) a marriage based primarily on sexual attraction has a very shaky foundation; and (c) marriage does not, in many cases, fully satisfy the sexual desires of both partners.

But only a part of the sexual function of marriage has to do with the sexual requirements of the individuals involved. As has already been indicated, many sociologists believe that marriage, insofar as it relates to sexuality, serves an important *social* function. Societies generally have laws, written or unwritten, intended to regulate sexual behavior (presumably in the interests of social welfare), and many of these laws are embodied in marriage vows and matrimonial restrictions. The topic of sex control will be considered more fully below. In the context of the present discussion, the reader should be reminded that the existence of a social regulation does not automatically signify that the regulation is necessary or even desirable for the individuals within a given society or for the society as a whole. Many laws, although never repealed, have become obsolete. Unknown to most of the citizenry and unenforced by the police, they survive as quaint relics of times past. As Kinsey *et al.* observed in 1953, "The current sex laws are unenforced and are unenforceable because they are too completely out of accord with the realities of human behavior."

Some may argue that the drift away from traditional sexual norms is at the root of our society's ills, but it is at least as reasonable to attribute those ills to the incompatibility of current norms with the social functions they are supposed to fulfill. For obvious reasons, evidence is hard to come by; but we may be able to gain some insights from accounts of times past. Thus, "the fact that the strict enforcement of coercive sanctions [on all sexual associations] was generally lacking for so long [during the Protestant Reformation] seems to show that they do not discharge a function as indispensable to social order as is sometimes represented by advocates."[7]

Unconvincing, too, is the contention that group cohesiveness is impossible in the absence of strict regulations against non-marital sexual activity. Dozens of societies have managed to perpetuate themselves in the absence of such restrictions. One might even maintain that increasing the range of possible sexual partners would have the salubrious effect of strengthening society by reducing frustration and broadening perspectives.

Few persons will deny that legal restraints are necessary to protect the physically helpless, the feeble-minded, the very young, and the psychotic from sexual abuse. Also, prohibitions against incest may be in the social interest. But with these exceptions, Havelock Ellis seems to have been quite correct in asserting that "the sexual act is of no more concern to the community than any other physiological act . . . . It is an impertinence, if not an outrage, to seek to inquire into it." (We may assume that by "inquire" Ellis was referring to meddling, rather than studying.) In the same passage, there appears one of Ellis' most picturesque comments: "Not what goes into the womb, but what comes out of it, concerns society."

Sex being an undesirable, irrational, and infrequent justification for marrying, we may turn to some of the other historically significant functions and see if any of these still have currency.

The Economic Function

As was suggested in Chapter I, ancient man and ancient woman may have initiated a marital partnership that was economically advantageous to both. But times have changed. Laundromats, supermarkets, old-age pensions, unemployment compensation, baby sitters, cotton mills, and countless other modern developments mean that neither husband nor wife is unexpendable in what may broadly be called the economic sphere. The woman who stays at home may constitute a relatively cheap source of domestic labor, but she is by no means indispensable. And the ever increasing opportunities for women to work outside the home make her less and less dependent, economically, upon her husband.

It is true, of course, that some women still marry as part of a bargain: "I'll sleep with you if you satisfy my economic needs." We have a name for such relationships.[8] And exploitation, even when it is mutual, cannot be regarded as a sound basis for marriage.

After pointing out that, from a purely economic standpoint, "getting married might well be considered an irrational choice of action," Greenfield went on to observe in 1965 that marriage serves an important economic function for the society at large. He is undoubtedly correct in asserting that the family, in the United States, constitutes the primary unit of consumption. But it is not at all clear that we therefore cannot do without the family.[9] As women continue to liberate themselves from the stereotyped role of consumer, we may expect a number of changes in the family structure and in other aspects of the social structure. Power will be more evenly distributed. Production will increase up to a point and then may level off, with an accompanying reduction in working hours for both men and women. The ultimate effects of these changes on the American family can only be guessed at, but there is certainly no reason to expect the collapse of our society or of its economic underpinnings.

One economic function that needs to be singled out for special mention has to do with the role marriage has played in controlling the nature of the labor force. Traditionally, when the bride was carried over the threshold, she was expected to stay put. Being a wife meant being a homemaker. Once safely married, the woman became considerably less threatening as a potential competitor in the job market. Males and females could thus join forces in support of marriage—not for the moral reasons they might claim, but for economic gain. Conventional marriage held out the promise of economic support for the woman, and at the same time provided a certain measure of job security and status security for the man. However, there were a few problems associated with this apparently cozy arrangement. First, its premises were not always valid; some husbands could not or would not provide economic security for their wives and for their increasingly expensive families, and some wives did obtain employment outside the home. Second, the arrangement failed to take into account that any attempt to deprive human beings of basic economic rights is both immoral and doomed to ultimate failure. (The foregoing considerations have been expressed in the past tense. Although the traditionalist viewpoint is by no means dead, the women's liberation movement is rapidly converting it into a deviant anachronism.)

Child-rearing

The child-rearing function of contemporary marriage has so many intricate ramifications that an entire chapter (Chapter IV) has been reserved for detailed analysis of this topic. It may be pointed out here, however, that to argue that individuals marry because they desire to have children makes sense only so long as there are pressures against unwed parenthood. And to argue that marriage is necessary in order to force parents to stay with and care for their offspring implies that without legal and social pressures, many parents would desert their children. One can only wonder what kind of upbringing can be provided by parents who take care of their children only because they are forced to. Would not a well-staffed institution be preferable? But more about this later.

Companionship

Although "companionship" may sometimes be used either as a euphemism or as a conscious or unconscious rationalization for sex, it is still worthy of separate comment. Those who feel that life without marriage would be intolerably lonely are tacitly admitting that they find themselves boring. What kind of companions can they be for someone else? Besides, those who desire or require steady companionship should be able to find it by simply living with the companion or companions of their choice. If they are unwilling to do so because of "what people will say," then it appears that the decision to marry is not the result of the desire for companionship so much as the fear of social disapproval.

Fear of social stigma is not, of course, the only deterrent to non-marital liaisons. There is also the fear of eternal damnation (see p. 50), and the fear of desertion. The latter is particularly likely to afflict those individuals so lacking in self-esteem that they doubt that anyone would remain with them except when under legal compulsion to do so. In cases such as these, marriage appears to be a form of emotional parasitism.

In the pages that follow, reference will occasionally be made to the idea that marriage is somewhat better suited to the female personality—as it has been molded by our society—than to the male personality. It is relevant, therefore, to report at this point Waetjen & Grambs's finding that females in our society "are more interested in and have greater need for close human relationships than males." (For an expression of the contrary opinion—that marriage is more attractive to males than to females—see Edwards' 1967 article.)

Security

Closely related to the need for companionship is the need for security. This term signifies different things to different people. For those who are chronologically or psychologically teen-agers, it may mean nothing more than the assurance that there will never be another dateless Saturday night. For others, marital security may mean a refuge from overbearing parents. Or it may mean financial security, or the comfort of knowing that there will always be a shoulder to cry on, or an ear that is more or less accessible. In any case, there is a strong presumption that the person who feels he has to marry in order to be secure is an insecure person. Martinson's study has shown that girls who reveal, on the basis of psychological tests, the condition of "ego deficiency" (lack of self-confidence, of realistic goals, and of inner security) are more likely to marry than those with strong egos. Similarly, another study, by Bernard, reports that single women appear to enjoy a higher level of mental health than do married women. (Is this because emotionally ill women are more likely to seek husbands, or because marriage is a cause of emotional illness? Probably both explanations need to be considered.) But marriage, alas, is unlikely to provide the permanent security so often expected of it. In fact, the dependency that so often characterizes the marriage of an insecure person may breed even more insecurity (see p. 123).

If this analysis is correct, the need for security, although a frequently cited reason for marrying, is not one that would be invoked by the individual who is already enjoying emotional security. Indeed, for such persons none of the reasons examined so far would be applicable.

Love

As has been mentioned, love was probably not among the original causes of marriage. A series of historical accidents, including the basically neurotic tradition of courtly love (see Askew's 1965 paper), has resulted in the glorification of love in the Western world. But cannot love be expressed and enjoyed outside of marriage? In fact, if love is the very desirable experience that the marriage-for-love advocates claim it is, then a relationship that lasts for as long as there is love should be far preferable to one that lasts for as long as there is life. (Divorce is a means of terminating a marriage whose foundations have crumbled, but its social and economic consequences are such that many people will prefer to remain in a loveless marriage.)

Bertrand Russell suggested in 1929 that "love is the principal means of escape from the loneliness which affects most men and women throughout the greater part of their lives." But why is loneliness so pervasive? Some writers, invoking the concept of existential loneliness, might maintain that being lonely is an inescapable part of the human condition. But I believe we must be careful to distinguish between the state of *aloneness* and the plight of *loneliness*. The former may well be an ultimate fact of human experience, but the awareness of this fact need not result in the unpleasant feelings that characterize loneliness. Rather than being viewed as universal and inevitable, loneliness may merely reflect the extent to which family life, with its stress on close human relationships, renders a person incapable of coping with the pressures of everyday life without the support of other people. And society's emphasis on marriage is such as to define the husband or wife as the logical and most desirable source of consolation. It appears, then, that we have the vicious circle of marriage contributing to the insecurities that impel people to marry, with the need for love emerging as little more than an infirmity contracted, as if by contagion, in the familial nest.

Another explanation for the prevalence and high valuation of love is related to what has been described above. Life consists largely of a series of decisions. We are virtually forced, simply in order to achieve some sort of adaptation to the world around us, to develop tentative ideas about right-wrong, beauty-ugliness, Democrat-Republican, coffee-tea, and innumerable other choice-points of varying degrees of importance and complexity. But we can almost never be sure of the correctness of our choices. Whenever a choice is made, other possibilities are rejected; and these other possibilities must have had *some* kind of appeal or no choice would have had to be made. Ordinarily, we are more eager to justify our choices than to change them. Unless we are unusually self-confident, we will seek such confirmation from other people. And the best confirmation is another person who has made the very same choices. (This may be one reason why some individuals so zealously attempt to change the opinions of others.) When a person with congruent life-patterns is found, that person becomes desirable as a source of self-esteem. And since that person's self-esteem is also being gratified, a reciprocal dependency develops. The two individuals, so much like each other, begin to "like" each other.[10] The bond between them will be especially strong if both of the foregoing aspirations (for a reduction in loneliness and for a confirmation of decisions made under conditions of uncertainty) are satisfied within the relationship.

In general, we may postulate that the more needs of Person A that are satisfied by Person B, the more important Person B will be for Person A. The resulting attachment, whether we choose to call it dependency or devotion or love, will be usually—perhaps inevitably—accompanied by the fear of losing this significant source of gratification. This fear, which is at the root of the pernicious emotion called jealousy, would be far less frequent if love were as unselfish as it is sometimes claimed to be. Jealousy appears to have two bases: feelings of inadequacy and feelings of proprietorship over another human being. Marriage makes this proprietorship "official," and thus forces both partners to be vigilant in order to reduce the chances of public humiliation (see Albert Ellis' comments, 1962).

Aside from fear, love may also have anger as a principal component. When one individual becomes increasingly dependent on another, mutual feelings of resentment may be expected to arise. The mixed feelings, the love-hate complex so apparent in our myths and dreams, may be the norm rather than the exception. "Pure love," unalloyed with destructive impulses, very possibly does not exist. Friedland has proposed that, disturbing though the idea may be, the ultimate goal of love may be the death of the beloved.

Also contributing to the development of affection is the desire for sexual pleasure. Many members of our society have apparently liberated themselves from the belief that sex should occur only within the confines of marriage, but large numbers continue to be influenced by the almost equally conservative dictum that sex must be accompanied by love. The sexually aroused individual, in order to avoid feelings of anxiety or guilt, is thus especially prone to fall in love.[11] More declarations of love have probably been made in parked cars than in any other location. Many of these are undoubtedly nothing more than seduction ploys,[12] but the role of self-seduction should not be underestimated.

And if to the pressures of sex and self-doubt are added the pressures emitted by the mass media, with their insistence that love, or lovableness, is the primary goal of life and that the love-free person is someone to be pitied, then it becomes obvious that only the most independent and secure individuals will find themselves able to feel comfortable in the absence of romantic entanglements.

One may conclude from these observations that (1) people should be able to enjoy a love relationship without having to get married, so long as they are psychologically strong enough to withstand social pressures; and (2) the *need*, as distinguished from the *ability*, to give and receive love, is a sign of immaturity or personal inadequacy. This latter point requires further comment, because it can be easily misunderstood. Although some writers have asserted that love is itself a state of pathology—"a psychic disease to be treated and cured"[13] — I believe that pathology enters the picture only when the individual has reached a state in which love has become a necessity if life is to be enjoyed. In such cases, love takes on the characteristics of an addiction. It becomes a symptom of, or perhaps a temporary palliative for, underlying emotional sickness.[14] As Michael Balint has put it, "There are three common dangers for a weak ego: psychosis...intoxication...falling in love."

In extreme cases, the individual may go so far as to "lose" himself, to abandon his own individuality, in favor of his beloved. Though extolled by some poets, this loss may be fraught with adverse consequences. Are we not already sufficiently de-individualized? If we had more self-esteem, would we still be so willing to lose our identities? "We are thus driven," writes Arthur Koestler, "to the unfashionable and uncomfortable conclusion that the trouble with our species is not an overdose of self-asserting aggression, but an excess of self-transcending devotion."

It should not be surprising, therefore, that, as Goode said in 1959, "many sociologists have disparaged it [romantic love] as a poor basis for marriage, or as immaturity." And yet, the American love-marriage complex continues to find expression, sometimes in the least expected places. For example, it is rather surprising to read, in Parsons & Bales's elaborately technical sociological description of family structure, the following unsupported statement: "The mature man can only love a woman who is really an adult, a full wife to him and mother to his children..."

As was pointed out earlier, the linkage of love and marriage is of fairly recent origin. One anthropologist concludes that it was not until the 1880's or 90's that there developed "the fantastic notion that one man and one woman should mate and after that be responsible for satisfying all of the other's significant emotional needs—obviously an impossible assignment."[15]

These comments on the nature of love are obviously far removed from the more lofty interpretations offered by many social philosophers and theologians. The discrepancy reflects the difference between what love "should" be, and the way it is actually experienced. There may be individuals whose love is free of the desire for total possession of, or by, another person; individuals whose love is firmly grounded in respect for the self and for the other; individuals for whom loving and being loved are not dire necessities. But who can deny that this ideal version of love is, more often than not, polluted by the quite unlofty pre-existing needs of the people concerned? One simple example may suffice. Suppose your spouse, returning home after an out-of-town trip, reports that he or she had had a casual sexual experience while away. If love is, as Heinlein put it, "that condition in which the happiness of another person is essential to your own," then it would be appropriate for you to respond, "Oh, I'm so glad. I hope you had fun." Although statistical evidence is lacking, it seems safe to say that such reactions are rather infrequent.

But what if the devaluation of love suggested in the foregoing paragraphs should prove to be invalid? Would we then be forced to acknowledge that marriage is of value because it fosters love? Not according to a recent analysis that concludes with the statement that monogamous marriage is so conducive to self-absorption that it destroys love, rather than enhancing it.[16]

Social Pressure

From the preceding discussion, the inference emerges that marriage provides a means for avoiding the social pressures that force one into marriage. This is not a particularly rational or elevating justification, but it may be the only one that truly applies.

It may be easy to criticize social pressures, but it is hard to discount them. The typical American is indoctrinated into the monogamous way of life. He sees marriage all around him. He hears, from parents and nearly everyone else in his environment, a continual emphasis on "when [not "if"] you get married..." The female child, especially, is subjected to insidious propaganda. Broderick's study revealed that about 95% of all the girls interviewed had already decided, by the age of twelve, to get married some day. What are the effects of this early emphasis on matrimony? Here is de Beauvoir's description:

> Parents still raise their daughter with a view to marriage rather than to furthering her personal development; she sees so many advantages in it that she herself wishes for it; the result is that she is often less specially trained, less solidly grounded than her brothers, she is less deeply involved in her profession. In this way she dooms herself to remain in its lower levels, to be inferior; and the vicious circle is formed: this professional inferiority reinforces her desire to find a husband.

For boys, the pressure is initially much less, so that de Beauvoir is probably correct in stating that "the girl in search of a husband is not responding to a masculine demand, she is trying to create one." Before long, however, the brainwashing techniques reach the male as well: As Cadwallader said in 1967, "His parents have been telling him that a little marriage poured over raw teenager yields instant maturity. They should know better."

These pressures not only force young people into marriages for which they may have neither need nor aptitude; the same pressures are also likely to create, in a considerable number of young people, guilt feelings before the final commitment is made. Albert Ellis, in 1949, pointed out the possibly dangerous discrepancy between society's emphasis on exclusivity in love relationships and the individual's experience of multiple romantic involvements.

When the dating years begin, the youngster is virtually forced to regard every member of the other sex—except those defined as ineligible because of marital or social status—as a prospective spouse. As the years pass, the pressures become less and less subtle. The girl, especially, is often made to feel that she has failed in college if she has not acquired a fiancé by the time she graduates. It is probable that an exceedingly large number of marriages are the direct or indirect results of threats, manipulations, insinuations, or bribes by parents who themselves had been pressured into matrimony.

Why are parents—so many of whom have been involved in divorces, annulments, permanent separations, or unhappy marriages that are being prolonged only because of a sense of duty to the children, fear of the adverse opinions of their equally distraught neighbors, submission to the dictates of the church, or sheer sloth—so eager to see their offspring tied in the bonds of matrimony? There are a number of possible answers.

In many cases, the parents are horrified by the prospect of illegitimate pregnancy. But it is unlikely that *every* pair of solicitous parents simply fears disgrace. Other parents may fervently wish to get their children out of the house as soon as possible, in order to lighten the financial and other burdens of child-care. Also, in many cases the parents may harbor secret doubts about the adequacy and desirability of their children (with accompanying misgivings about their own failures as parents), or they may fear that others harbor such doubts—the only certain remedy for which is an early and fruitful marriage.

I have not mentioned the possibility that marriage-pushing parents may be genuinely interested in promoting the happiness and welfare of their children. It is doubtful that such altruism occurs very frequently. Psychoanalytic case studies abound with accounts of marriage-pushers (along with food-pushers, money-pushers, and love-pushers) who—beneath the smiling or tearful masks of parental love—are ceaselessly attempting to dominate or humiliate their children. The reasons for this widespread hostility are beyond the scope of this chapter; suffice it to say that the incidence of unwanted pregnancies, of births so painful that the mother retains a lifelong hatred of the innocent cause of her discomfort (the father often sharing this antipathy), of the bitter disappointment of bearing a son instead of a daughter or vice versa, of the unreasoning anger when one's child grows up to be neither a movie star nor a baseball player nor an Einstein, of the deep resentments arising from unpleasant messes in toilet training, less-than-perfect breast-feeding, interrupted sleep, reductions in freedom, etc., etc., is so great that we should not be at all surprised to find unmixed parental love as rarely as we do.

Not everyone succumbs to the pro-marriage pressures of parents, although it is possible that such pressures play an important role in perhaps the majority of marriages. It goes without saying, of course, that these pressures may be effectively operating despite the denials, or even unawareness, of either parent or child.

. When parents exert pressure on their children, they are reflecting not only their own needs but also society's pervasive emphasis on marriage. It is to these more general social pressures that we now direct our attention.

As Kenkel has written, "If it were possible to obtain completely honest answers about the matter, we might find that in our society the wish to conform to group standards, to live as most adults live, is a stronger motivating force for marriage than is realized." The social pressures have become so ubiquitous that they are not always recognized as such. But the income tax deductions and other financial benefits accorded to "family men," the lower likelihood of being drafted into wartime military service, and the increased chances of advancement in certain professional fields are all unmistakable instances of how the United States attempts to persuade its citizens to marry.

These pressures are not, of course, devoid of historical roots, nor are they confined to any one country. Baber writes that "Athens considered celibacy a crime against the household gods, Sparta took away certain civil rights from bachelors,[17] and Rome made bachelors ineligible for inheritances." (He adds, significantly, "Tacitus declared that these measures did little to increase marriage.") Contemporary carry-overs of these and other pressures are apparent in most European countries: until quite recently, as Baber points out, there was a bachelors' tax in France and Germany, while in Germany and Italy marriage was a prerequisite for political advancement. And Lewinsohn describes an unwritten law in England, dating from Victorian times, preventing the accreditation of any diplomat who has been divorced.

The prevalence and intensity of social influence are well expressed by Malinowski in his 1960 article: "The attainment of a full tribal status is always a powerful motive for marriage."[18] Although perhaps somewhat overstated, his comment still requires us to inquire into the reasons for society's concern over the private behavior of its members. Social pressure toward marriage constitutes a mighty and almost irresistible stream. By exploring some of its tributaries, we may be able to reach an understanding of its sources and of the extent of its strength.

One form of social pressure that undoubtedly serves to elevate the marriage rate is the pressure against unwed motherhood.[19] According to the U.S. Department of Health, Education, and Welfare, at least one-third of all firstborn children in the United States are conceived before marriage. Although we cannot conclude that none of these marriages would have occurred without the instigation of pregnancy, it does seem reasonable to suggest that *some* of them would not have occurred, and that *many* of them would not have occurred when they did. In any case, statistics show that marriages involving pregnant brides are especially likely to end in divorce.[20]

Potent as the pressure against illegitimacy may be, it seems to be becoming a less compelling reason to marry. The *New York Times* reported on November 19, 1967 (p. 36) that one out of every 15 babies born in the United States is born to an unwed mother. (Such a ratio is probably on the conservative side, in view of the large number of illegitimate births that go unreported.) Clearly, many couples have children without getting married, just as many couples get married without having children. Social recognition of the increasing number of illegitimate births—the number has tripled in the past 25 years—is reflected in the laws of many states asserting that every child is the legitimate offspring of his natural parents.

One should also bear in mind that pregnancy becomes a progressively less frequent motive for marriage as the wonders of modern science make undesired conceptions progressively rarer. The fact that the marriage rate has not declined, despite the increasing availability of contraceptives, suggests that pregnancy, or the fear thereof, should probably no longer be viewed as a *major* determinant of the pro-marriage pressures that continue to be exerted.

Some of the strongest of these pressures are religious in origin. It is of more than passing interest, therefore, to note that Christianity's active advocacy of marriage is a fairly recent development. Saturninus, an early Church leader, believed, according to Hippolytus, that marriage and procreation were the work of the devil. St. Jerome believed, May reports, that marriage could be tolerated only because it provided the world with virgins. And an edict of the Council of Trent (1545-1563) specifically asserted that virginity was preferable to marriage. As late as 1724, Father Lafitau, in the first systematic book on social anthropology, declared that marriage was a "shameful" necessity.

But a shift did come about. The change probably had multiple determinants, but two factors must have been especially important. First, there was the realization of the fact that the steady propagation of new generations of adherents was necessary in the competition for souls—hence the strong sanctions against religious intermarriage. A passage in the marriage service of the Church of England[21] declares that the first purpose of marriage is "the procreation of children, to be brought up in the fear and nurture of the Lord, and to the praise of His holy name." (The second purpose is to prevent fornication, and the third is "mutual society, help, and comfort.") Similarly, in the Catholic Church, marriage's role as a baby-producer is amply indicated by the official position concerning contraception and by numerous pronouncements to the effect that, in the words of Francis de Sales, "procreation of children is the first and principal end of marriage."

The other obvious stake that religion has in marriage is the regulation of sexual behavior. As St. Paul had said, "It is better to marry than to burn."[22] If sex could not be completely eliminated, it could at least be confined within the narrow limits of lifelong monogamy. But even marital sexuality was viewed with misgivings. May points out that the second archbishop of Canterbury set a 40-day period of penance to follow marriage, and that Anglo-Saxon Church law forbade marital relations on Sundays, Wednesdays, Fridays, fast days, and during religious festivals. Clement of Alexandria stipulated, as cited in M. M. Hunt, that sexual relations between husband and wife should occur only at night, and never after returning from market. The still-current downgrading by the Catholic Church of sexual intercourse undertaken for recreation rather than procreation points in the same direction. As Hunt has pointed out, "Christianity forbade the separate gratification of the desires for sex, love, and marriage, but made it impossible to enjoy them together."[23]

An understanding of the early Church's position concerning sexual morality requires consideration of some of the concurrent social forces at work. For example, the Essene sects that were among the immediate precursors of Christianity displayed quite varied orientations toward marriage. Briffault mentions in *The Mothers* that some of these sects permitted trial marriage, which was solemnized only if the woman proved fertile. But May reports that other Essene groups viewed sexuality— including marital sexuality—as bordering on the obscene: "Marriage was held in aversion, although many Essenes married, believing themselves enjoined to procreation, even at the cost of pollution." May goes on to present evidence that Jesus came from one of these latter groups.

Christianity also has roots in the older Hebraic civilization, with its own emphatic support of marriage, as outlined in the Jewish code of laws.[24] Judaism's attitude toward sexual behavior cannot be easily categorized. Although the ancient Hebrew laws did not provide for punishment of voluntary sexual relations between the unmarried, many segments of Hebrew law and tradition strongly discouraged sexual freedom. All meetings in private between men and women were prohibited, "unchaste conduct" was considered to be "among the most heinous offences against God and society," and ritual circumcision was interpreted as a means of weakening the penis in order to prevent sexual excesses. Nevertheless, celibacy was frowned upon, the sex drive being viewed as an "evil inclination without which no man would build a home and marry."[25] The apparent paradox is explained, in part, by the fact that many sexual restrictions had grounds other than sexual morality, as narrowly conceived. For example, May states that "the rule of Exodus as to seduction stands not among the laws of personal injury but at the close of a list of cases of pecuniary compensations for injury to property"—a position that may have been foreshadowed by the view which Havelock Ellis attributes to "most savage and barbarous societies," that adultery was "an illegitimate appropriation of property." Regardless of the rationale for these restrictions on sexuality (which date from the seventh century, B.C.), Kinsey, *et al.* make it clear, in their 1953 report, that there can be little doubt of their continuing impact:

> Jewish sex codes were brought over into Christian codes by the early adherents of the Church, including St. Paul, who had been raised in the Jewish tradition on matters of sex. The Catholic sex code is an almost precise continuation of the more ancient Jewish code. For centuries in medieval Europe, the ecclesiastic law dominated on all questions of morals and subsequently became the basis for the English common law, the statute laws of England, and the laws of the various states of the United States. This accounts for the considerable conformity between the Talmudic and Catholic codes and the present-day statute law on sex.

Christianity has Classical (chiefly Platonic) roots as well; and these, too, had anti-sexual components. May points out that "Empedocles and Diocles had thought that semen came from the brain and spinal marrow and that excessive copulation injured the senses and the spine. This notion was adopted by Plato," and Kelsen recalls Plato's assertion that sexual intercourse was philosophically acceptable only if its goal was reproduction. Plato also felt, as put forward in *The Statesman*, that intercourse without procreative intent was a form of murder,[26] and that sexual reproduction would not occur in paradise.[27] Such thinking had enormous influence. According to May, "It is no exaggeration to say that neo-Platonic dualism, in the cloak of Christian asceticism, was handed down by Augustine in English tradition and English law." The continuity from ancient Greek pre-scientific philosophy to the presumably more

enlightened modern era is well expressed by Jean
Mayer:

> Saint Augustine, rising from a Manichaean
> background and a personally unhappy sexual
> history, defined the purpose of Christian mar-
> riage as procreation, with abstinence permissi-
> ble by mutual consent. This basis of the Chris-
> tian marriage, unmodified by Thomas Aquinas
> or the medieval theologians, unmodified by
> Luther (an Augustinian, very much attached
> to the pattern of the order), was to survive far
> into the twentieth century.

It would be quite incorrect to conclude that all Greek
thinking was puritanical. On the contrary, sexual in-
discretions were the object of attention only when they
violated the Greek ideals of justice and moderation. The
Greeks had no word for chastity. When the early Chris-
tians wished to express this concept in Greek, they had
to use the term *agneia*, which referred to the rites of
mourning—including sexual abstinence—that were employed to appease the gods and spirits. Thus, in Briffault's 1930 formulation, Christianity converted, at least
verbally, a general abstinence from pleasure on specific
religious occasions into a particularized emphasis on the
year-round value of chastity.

   We are getting closer now to the crucial question: of
all the forms of human behavior, why has Christianity
(along with many other religions) chosen sexual behavior
as a major object of suppression? Perhaps a need was
felt by the founders of the various religions to de-
animalize the human species. After all, if man was un-
ique among all living things in his possession of a soul
and his apprehension of God, then the fewer links there

were between our exalted selves and our soul-less fellow creatures, the more likely would it be that religion could establish a foothold. But even the powers of religion could not eradicate most of our resemblances to the rest of the animal kingdom: we continue to eat, to breathe, to sleep, to excrete, to die. Among the very few animal attributes that could be tampered with were sexual behavior and nudity. Sex, within marriage, became either a sacrament or a bit of nastiness to be endured only when absolutely necessary; nudity became sinful.

There appears to be little logic behind this anti-sexual position. The fact that the human animal is an animal does not negate the many attributes (e.g., symbol-making) that differentiate man from the rest of the animal kingdom. Indeed, one of the most striking and elevating comments that we can make about ourselves is that we have gone as far as we have within the confines of our inescapable heritage. Ironically, as L.K. Frank pointed out in 1954, religious suppression of sexual behavior includes an unintentional animalizing aspect: "One of our strongest traditions is that human sex is moral and legitimate only for procreation, which is essentially the subhuman 'barnyard' pattern of episodic copulation for fertilization..."

Two conclusions emerge from this account of contemporary religion's stress on marriage. First, religion uses marriage as a means of ensuring future adherents through the production and indoctrination of offspring, thus creating what almost amounts to a conspiracy to reduce the possibility of independent thinking in future generations. Second, religion uses marriage as a vehicle for suppressing sexual behavior, thereby perpetuating a set of ancient taboos based largely on fear and ignorance.

Clearly, religious pressures—expressed via the home, the community, or the church itself—are important determinants of many persons' decisions to marry. But a marriage undertaken in blind obedience to a religious requirement is far removed from a relationship based on mutual respect and affection. Instead, such a marriage closely resembles a savage rite, in which husband, wife, and progeny are the unthinking victims.[28]

Religious allegiances are probably weaker now than in times past, and some readers may object that I have unduly emphasized the practical importance of the Judeo-Christian advocacy of marriage. But considerable numbers of people continue to be governed by their traditional religious beliefs. For example, 35% of this author's 1970 sample of female college students included "religious or ethical considerations" in their list of reasons for wanting to get married. Also, it should be repeated here (see p. 48) that religion-based pressures toward marriage have become absorbed by our secular laws, so that, in Hefner's words, "the religious views of a portion of a society are forced upon the rest of it—through governmental coercion—whether they are consistent with the personal conviction or practice of the individual or not. . . .Incredible as it should seem, and despite all constitutional guarantees to the contrary, we do not enjoy a true separation of church and state in the United States today."

Another form of social pressure, intertwined with those already discussed, has to do with the important role marriage has played in the history of the United States. From almost the beginning, Baber points out, families and the American way of life have seemed virtually inseparable:

> The New England settlers came mostly from families, and a high premium was set on family life from the first. . . .In several colonies, bachelors paid special taxes. All were expected to

marry....As the settlers pushed farther west,
the frontier life favored early marriage more
than ever. Without the companionship of a
wife in his lonely cabin and deprived of her
own sturdy help as well as that of the sons she
might bear him, the bachelor's outlook was a
rigorous one. The unmarried woman's lot was
still less enviable, for frequently she was little
better than a servant in the home of her parents or relatives, with little individuality allowed her....One could not afford to pass up
many opportunities to escape the dread of
spinsterhood.

Similarly, James Truslow Adams has indicated the extent
to which the family came to dominate early American
life: "Under the conditions of frontier existence the family tended to become greatly strengthened as a social,
economic, and even military unit." And Baber also informs us that the Dutch settlers in New York "frowned
upon bachelors" as much as did their English counter-
parts. Spinsterhood was also frowned upon in colonial
America: Reed states that, "A young unmarried woman
of 18 or 20 was looked upon as an old maid."

Today, although the previously important economic
and military functions of the family are becoming or
have become obsolete, the tradition of "marriage for all"
persists. Indeed, the acceptance of marriage is a sign
of good citizenship. As recently as 1911, the Women's
Homestead Association, in Boston, passed the following
resolution: "Resolved, that we appeal to the law-abiding
family men who are voters not to cast their votes for
the bachelor candidates" (*New York Herald Tribune*, November 1, 1911, p. 1). Even worse, to decide against
marriage for oneself is to run the risk of being accused
of emotional illness.[29]

So, although the argument that "we in America have always had marriage" is no more pertinent than saying that "we in America have always had crime," historical pressure combines with the other pressures that have been discussed, leaving all but the most independent members of the population virtually helpless when it comes to making an intelligent decision about how the 50 years of one's mature life are to be spent. Clearly, Hobart's statement that "the family persists because people want and need the family" explains nothing and obscures the important issues involved.

A more penetrating analysis has recently been offered by Herbert Otto: "This most ingenious artificial institution, grafted onto certain basic human needs (material security, sex, companionship, the protection of children, etc.) serves those who control society: it is a way to 'divide and rule.' Because of that and the preservation of property within the narrow limits of the family circle, the Establishment, to promote its own interests, tries to impose the concept of the conventional family through school, home, mass media, pulpit, etc., not to mention the violence of the law."

Perhaps this section can best be concluded by referring to Berger & Kellner's in-depth, and generally favorable, analysis of marriage, which asserts that "the compulsion to legitimate the stabilized marital world, be it in psychologistic or in traditional religious terms, is another expression of the precariousness of its construction."

Other Individual Functions

A number of other psychological needs, aside from the need to conform to cultural expectations, may lead to marriage. The Oedipus complex, for example, while probably not so widespread as Freud claimed, remains a powerful motivational source in our culture. A man pushing out of awareness the forbidden sexual desires he feels toward his mother may choose for a wife a woman similar in age, name, physical appearance, or habits to the initially desired bedmate. (As might be predicted, the sex life in such marriages is often disastrous: after finding a mother-symbol to sleep with, the man may be inhibited by the onrushing feelings of guilt and fear that the similarity elicits.) Or, if the individual is somewhat less successful in repressing his incestuous drives, he may, consciously or otherwise, set about to marry someone as *different* as possible from his mother—again failing to recognize the individuality of whatever woman he selects. (Similar forces may, of course, be operating within the woman.) Without the urgent need to resolve these unresolved tensions, many persons might never marry at all.

Some writers in the mental health field have argued that marriage is of value because it promotes and maintains such positively valued traits as maturity, stability, and a sense of responsibility. This assertion will be challenged later (see page 124), but even if it were true, it is equally true that the person who is already mature is unlikely to look to marriage as a locus for maturation. And there is always the risk that the irresponsible person will infect spouse and children with his irresponsibility. Even Denis de Rougemont, a passionate defender of marriage, makes the following large concession: "I feel indeed that every one of the extremely varied objections that the finest minds have ever urged against it [marriage] is still valid....Inasmuch as when taken one by one most human beings of both sexes are either rogues or neurotics, why should they turn into angels the moment they are paired?"

Marriage is a far cry from psychotherapy. Often enough, as psychiatrist Lawrence Kubie pointed out in 1956, "the choosing of a mate is one of the most confused steps a human being takes in life." Nevertheless, marriage may be useful the way a crutch is useful, enabling the psychologically handicapped to function while remaining crippled. And although excessive reliance on crutches may result in atrophy of the affected parts, it would be unrealistic and inhuman to advocate the total elimination of crutches. It is for a quite similar reason that the reader will find no advocacy of the total abolition of marriage in these pages.

Finally, we may consider the assertion in *Open Marriage*, by O'Neill & O'Neill, that marriage provides the "structure" that human beings require in their interpersonal relations. This is a difficult statement to interpret, because "structure" is one of those simple-sounding terms that obscure more than they describe. Strictly speaking, most sociologists would probably say that *any* interaction involving two or more members of the same society is bound to have a structure based on culturally determined, shared expectations. Many psychologists would deny the contention that people *need* structure; or, if they accepted the statement, they would go on to point out that structure is something we impose upon a situation, rather than something inherent in the situation. From this latter perspective, we see that any relationship between human beings, whether it be a one-night stand or a lifelong marriage, is a sort of ink-blot test, the structure of which will be perceived according to the needs and past experiences of the perceiver. What, then, is meant by those who maintain that nonmarital relationships lack structure? They are presumably referring to a particular type of structure, characterized by relative permanence and by an explicit, legally binding set of reciprocal agreements.[30] There can be no denying that this sort of arrangement is necessary or desirable for some people, freeing them from the day-to-day worry as to whether the relationship will continue, and enabling them to relax in their dealing with one another. But such arrangements may be oppressively restrictive to others, who can function better within relationships that are structured differently (e.g., non-marital relationships). Somewhat inconsistently, the O'Neills acknowledge that marriage would *not* be necessary "if all of us had reached a stage of human development that assured mutual responsibility and trust between all people," and that a woman could "lead a life of fulfillment" without marrying, if she had educational, sexual, and economic freedom. These exceptions suggest either that some people can do without structure, or that the structure can be obtained outside of marriage. The person who invokes the notion of structure to justify the statement, "People need marriage," may really be saying nothing more than, "*I* need marriage."

Other Social Functions

One frequently encounters the statement that our whole economic, or political, or social system depends on marriage, and that marriage is therefore necessary if our way of life is to be preserved. Even so august a body as the United Nations has endorsed this position.[31] However, no convincing evidence supports the contention.

Statements such as Coppinger & Rosenblatt's "Societies generally function more smoothly with stable marriage" leave several questions begged or unanswered. Is the statement anti-divorce (because divorces signify unstable marriages), or pro-divorce (because if "unstable" marriages can be quickly terminated, there would be a higher proportion of "stable" marriages)? Is it really true that unstable marriages *cause* societies to run less smoothly, or—as was suggested at the beginning of this chapter—could it not be that the unstable marriages are *consequences* of social changes that have made marriage a less and less effective means of satisfying human needs? The possibility should be seriously considered that Western society is outgrowing marriage, just as it outgrew the horse and buggy (and some readers may still recall the outraged cries that America's economy required the horse and buggy). And even if it could be established that stable marriages are better, for our present society, than are unstable marriages, this finding would neither mean nor imply that stable marriages are better than no marriages at all. Moreover, there are more than a few malcontents who would argue that the preservation of our society as it is currently operating is not a particularly worthy objective.

It is not enough to claim, as has been done in this chapter, that there may no longer be any sound reasons for marrying. There is another side of the coin, having to do with the good reasons for *not* marrying. But first we must consider the children.

III

Child-bearing and Child-rearing

FOR MANY PEOPLE, the concepts "marriage" and "family" are virtually inseparable; to marry *means* to have a family. While not everyone makes this equation, the fact remains that many (perhaps most) individuals who marry in our culture have, as one of their motives, a desire for children. Also, the social pressures in favor of marriage are focusing less and less on its economic and sexual aspects, and more and more on the alleged responsibility of each of us to produce and "socialize" the citizens of tomorrow. Surely, if the reproductive and socializing functions of marriage are that important, the institution would have to continue even if it were otherwise obsolete. But, just as surely, if marriage is *not* required for these functions, then the ultimate justification for marriage might well begin to crumble.

This chapter will examine in detail the desire of men and women to have children. In the following chapter, after the importance of children to parents has been discussed, an attempt will be made to evaluate the importance of parents to children.

"I wanted to have children." A whole host of motives and sub-motives lie concealed beneath this familiar explanation of the decision to marry. Ignoring for the present the debatable and vulnerable assumption underlying this explanation—that children outside of marriage would be unthinkable—let us try to ascertain what it means to "want" to have children. It means a great many things, some of them quite uninspiring. In the words of English & Pearson, the authors of a well-known, and rather conservative, volume on mental health,

> . . .we should realize that a great many adults have children just because it is being done, or because they are ignorant about contraceptives, or because they want to gain some degree of immortality through their children. We should not delude ourselves into thinking that the majority of parents have children because they love them, or that their main goal in life as parents is to help the oncoming generation to adapt to and enrich society generally.

Let us discuss some of these motives somewhat more systematically.

Anthropologists have provided us with a great deal of evidence to support the thesis that, in various parts of the world, the desire for children is largely economically based. For example, Nathan Miller's statement that "the parents' urge is first of all a utilitarian and selfish one . . . . Children are man's most precious possession in the simpler society," is followed by examples from more than twenty cultures, ranging from the Hottentots to the ancient Hebrews. This motive is an important one to reckon with today, as reflected in Spengler's recent proposal for lowering the birth rate by providing guaranteed social security benefits and old-age pensions to members of societies that have customarily viewed offspring as necessary for these purposes.

Of course, the fact that economic considerations are of such importance in so many parts of the world, among so many primitive and not-so-primitive societies, does not necessarily mean that similar motives are involved in our own culture. At least with respect to farmers and home-based skilled artisans in the United States, there is reason to believe that the desire to have children (primarily, sons) in order to keep the wealth and the business in the family is, though scantily documented, not at all uncommon. In general, however, the economic motive seems to be losing its importance: as Baber points out, "It has been recognized for some time that in this country, with its rapid trend toward urbanization, children are becoming an economic liability instead of the asset they used to be." But at the same time time, as Moore has suggested, the United States continues to be influenced by the Puritan ethic, with its emphasis on productivity. The forces that impel us to work in order to produce more and more wealth may be implicitly defining the marriage-bed as just another factory.

Of course, not all of the instigations for parenthood are economic in nature. A number of motives revolve around the desire for domestic felicity. Sumner states that among the Gilbert Islanders, a woman's pregnancy was the usual excuse for husband and wife to leave the home of oppressive parents and in-laws. Among the Masai, Basuto, and Bantu (and in many other societies, past and present), according to Miller's investigations, wives can be divorced for sterility, so that child-bearing becomes a means of ensuring the continuation of the marriage. Reasons such as these undoubtedly occur among ourselves, although they usually escape notice—and perhaps consciousness—behind a veneer of more acceptable motives. One study, by Despert, does make explicit reference to the fact that some pregnancies represent attempts to resolve family problems. (As will be noted later, such attempts frequently backfire.)

Another motive for reproduction may be, on the father's part, to prove virility. As Miller puts it, in regard to certain African societies, "He who fails in this respect is regarded...as something less than a man." Stycos has also reported this way of thinking for Puerto Rico, and it is, of course, not uncommon in our own country. The motive is, in fact, such a prevalent one that it gains a place in Klineberg's list of the five chief reasons men have for wanting children (the others being economic, religious, the desire for immortality, and the influence of social pressures). The parallel superstition, that motherhood is the indispensable sign of womanhood, is probably at least as widespread. Within the context of our otherwise sophisticated society, these beliefs seem to reflect a combination of ignorance and insecurity.

As was true for marriage itself, one motive for having children may be related to the many rewards that a grateful society bestows upon parents. Income tax exemptions, draft deferments, and the like are probably of greater influence to some people than is generally acknowledged. According to Groves, "childbearing has formerly been one of the strongest traditions from which even the modern woman has not so thoroughly escaped as to make any declaration concerning the desire for children that is certain to be free from social coercion."[1] The social coercion is alarmingly effective. Levinson's survey indicated that many women decide to have children simply to "get it over with" or because "it's the thing to do." In such cases, it may be appropriate to apply the label, "status child," to denote, in Margaret Mead's words (1949) "a child that merely gives the parents the status of having had a child." Clearly, it is not only within "primitive" societies (e.g., the Nandi, Baganda, and Bakongo, as cited by Miller) that the childless woman is ridiculed by the community.

And in those cases in which ridicule is not apparent, other forms of social pressure may still express themselves. Whyte has reported that childless couples find it "almost impossible" to adjust to life in some suburban communities because of the child-centered emphasis in conversations and friendship patterns. If any manage to escape these informal influences, there remains the powerful voice of "expert" opinion: as Dykstra points out, "Even writers of treatises on the family are more inclined to portray the voluntarily childless as abnormal. The display of fertility in the United States is clearly regarded as honorable." Parsons' assertion, in *Family, socialization, and interaction process*, that the maternal role is helpful, or even essential, for the establishment of the woman's "personality equilibrium" is a particularly noteworthy example of the authoritative advocacy of motherhood. The statement, however, is quite unpersuasive, being based on (a) Freudian concepts of doubtful validity, and (b) a patriarchal view of society that is far less acceptable now than it was two decades ago. Furthermore, even if Parsons' position were to be confirmed, it could not be taken as an eternal verity; it would merely reflect how the current social emphasis on family life can adversely affect those who deviate from the norm.

As has been mentioned (p. 11), society's intense emphasis on reproduction has two bases: the requirements for constant replenishment of the population and for the inculcation of traditional social norms into each new generation. (This latter goal may be one explanation for society's insistence on *legitimate* children, the assumption being that parents must be present and must acknowledge their parental obligations if they are to be effective in training their children to be good citizens.)

The massive impact of the social, religious, and economic factors described here and in the preceding chapter may obscure some of the other, more mundane, reasons that impel some people to reproduce. Thus the desire to escape from boredom, the need for an excuse to avoid outside employment, etc., have not yet received sufficient documentation to warrant extended comment.[2] Suffice it to say that such reasons can be compellingly important despite their apparent triviality, and can pave the way for the exploitative use of the young child, in utter disregard of the child's own individuality.[3]

What kinds of people are most likely to want to be parents? If this analysis is correct, they would include those least able to resist social pressures and least able to find satisfaction in life via their own inner resources. Not surprisingly, women with low self-concepts have been found to have larger families than women with high self-concepts.[4] Perhaps the central consideration here is that of *power*. The woman who feels powerless is especially likely to succumb to the blandishments of our nationwide fertility cult and is especially likely to welcome a baby over whom she can exercise control. Likewise, the insecure man who feels that his power is being threatened will be particularly eager to keep his wife pregnant and home-bound. Stoller has perceptively noted the significance of the power motive in family settings: "It is, therefore, the needs of the parents which are ultimately served by their own devotion and service to their children; by sharing in their offspring's lives, parents can serve a part of themselves never completely dead, but so often dormant: their own child-self. In addition, parents require the sense of importance given them when the children acknowledge the central role they play in their lives by reflecting back to them the introjection of parental values."[5] This latter point helps to explain the basically progress-inhibiting nature of the family structure as it exists in our society.

These motives are all rather uninspiring. What about the more comforting idea that it is "instinctive" or "human nature" to want children? Since this idea has such wide currency, it deserves to be examined closely. First, for the sake of clarity, a terminological note is necessary. The so-called parental instinct may be divided into two categories, the paternal and the maternal; and the latter may itself by subdivided into the pre-maternal (the desire to have children) and the post-maternal (the affection and protectiveness felt for one's children).

The many animal species in which the father displays indifference or lethal hostility to his offspring, the many human societies in which the father shows no sign of devotion to his children, the large number of males in child-centered Western societies who take a dim view of parenthood,[6] and the utter absence of anything resembling a physiological basis for paternal behavior combine to render extremely doubtful the existence of a paternal instinct. Even those writers who maintain that most human behavior has instinctive roots are generally quite unwilling to place "fathering" in this category.

But while the existence of a paternal instinct is rejected by most students of animal and human behavior, considerable controversy continues to surround the female form of this alleged instinct. When a young girl expresses a longing to have children, or when a woman states that she intends to marry because she desires to have children, a pre-maternal drive is being manifested. The question is, is this admittedly strong drive instinctive, or is it the result of learning? Once again, Klineberg's criteria for instincts can be invoked.

It is rather difficult to apply, in this instance, the criterion of continuity with animals. Being unable to resort to interviewing, we must proceed largely by inference and speculation in trying to establish whether or not sub-human animals possess a desire for offspring. One conclusion emerges: such a drive, if it exists, has never been detected. No example of animal behavior can be definitely attributed to the "goal" of producing offspring. It is a safe bet that copulation among lower species is not motivated by a pre-parental drive. Nor is there any evidence that nests are built "in order to" provide shelter for the young.

The criterion of organic basis, on the other hand, is satisfied. The reproductive apparatus of the female is known to function, both before and during pregnancy, so as to maximize the likelihood of propagation. Also, the existence of such organs as the uterus makes the organic basis of child-bearing undeniable.

Application of the universality criterion yields strikingly negative results. The number of women in our own culture who have no desire for children is too great to be dismissed as "the exception that proves the rule." And even if the argument (a quite unsupported one) is raised that these women are psychologically deviant, we are still confronted with the fact that there are cultures in which the majority of women express a thorough distaste for children, regularly practice abortion, and in general display none of the characteristics one would expect if the pre-maternal drive were a part of "human nature."[7] A catalog of examples would be unduly lengthy, but the following may be considered as representative. Schneider tells us that the women of Yap, up to the age of 30, "did not want children because they would no longer be free to fall in and out of love, to attract lovers, to have and break off affairs at will, to practice the elaborate games of love and sociability that appeal to young Yap men and women." In Rome, Kenkel states, after the Punic Wars, children were "considered a burden and expense," and "remaining childless came to have a positive advantage," and Zimmerman affirms that, in rural Gaul, "means were even sought to force people to have children." A series of Julian Laws (18 B.C. to 9 B.C.), described by M. Hunt, was designed to increase the birth rate of the upper classes: bachelors, spinsters, and childless wives could no longer inherit, mothers of three or more children received special legal privileges, and the men with the largest number of children were given political preference. Such measures would hardly seem necessary if reproduction were instinctive.

Turning now to abortion, no claim can be made that every intentional termination of pregnancy is proof that the pre-maternal instinct does not exist. In many cases, such as illegitimate or physically dangerous pregnancies, it may be preferable to accept the hypothesis that pre-maternal needs do exist but are obscured by more pressing considerations. However, careful note should be made, in the following group of examples, of the many relatively trivial functions that have been served by abortion in various societies. Among the Dobu of New Guinea, as Fortune states, women had abortions because they feared that having a child would interfere with their attractiveness. Miller points out that Akamba women intentionally aborted so that their dancing would not be curtailed. An 1891 study by Codrington reports that the women in German Melanesia practiced abortion in order to avoid child-rearing chores, to preserve their youthful appearance, to avoid their husbands' suspicions of infidelity, or to spite their husbands. The women of New Hebrides employed abortion for "egoistic reasons," according to Sumner, and he further states that the Ka-

diveo of Paraguay "are perishing largely through abortion" because the women dislike work, wish to make their
horseback life easier, and are afraid of being left behind
by their husbands. According to Sumner's summary,
"abortion and infanticide are so nearly universal in savage life, either as egoistic policy or group policy, that
exceptions to the practice of these vices are noteworthy
phenomena." (Noteworthy, too, is Sumner's use of the
term "vice"—certainly not what one would expect from
an author who contributed so much to the idea of cultural relativism.) In a somewhat more recent ethnographic survey, George Devereaux concludes that "there
is every indication that abortion is an absolutely universal
phenomenon, and that it is impossible even to construct
an imaginary social system in which no woman would
ever feel at least impelled to abort." This generalization
appears to hold up quite well, although the exception of
Nazi Germany, which, Millett points out, totally banned
both abortion and contraception, should not be forgot-
ten.

In Japan, where abortion is now legal, relatively easy
to obtain, and inexpensive (seldom costing more than
$15),[8] the *New York Times* of May 28, 1963 (p. 18) re-
ports that there are as many abortions as live births.
Tietze states that about one million abortions are per-
formed per year in the United States, and Gebhard *et
al.* found that more than 20% of their large sample
of married women had at least one induced abortion.
These numbers may be expected to increase dramatically
as a result of recent legislative and judicial decisions.

Nor is abortion the only indicator of anti-natalist sentiment. The instinct hypothesis is also difficult to reconcile
with the widespread use of contraceptive devices and
practices. Contraception is by no means of recent origin.
An Egyptian medical document dating from about 1850

B.C. mentions women using certain gummy substances to prevent conception; and primitive women, de Lys reports, would sometimes thrust a ball of freshly plucked leaves into the vagina, for the same purpose. Zimmerman states that, in Athens, in the second century B.C., "the decline in parent-child relations can be measured. . . by the rise of the common use of birth control to an extreme resulting in childlessness and the depopulation of the native families."

Despite the increasing use of abortion and contraception, we cannot conclude that all babies are born wanted by their parents. Because of legal, ethical, cultural, religious, psychological, or financial impediments to effective birth control, a large number of undesired babies continue to be born. For the United States, Jaffe & Guttmacher have suggested the figure of 850,000 unwanted births per year. Rather surprisingly, in view of the presumably higher degree of sophistication possessed by the parents, studies of college marriages reveal that only about one-third of the pregnancies are planned.[9]

As a final indicator of the frequent insubstantiality of the pre-parental drive, we may refer to a group of studies, summarized by Hurlock, suggesting that the "desire for children is generally strongest among women who have no children. The romanticized concept of parenthood, after the arrival of the first child, often gives way to a more realistic one."

I am not claiming that there are no women with deep-seated urges to have children. But this yearning clearly seems to result from early training and social pressures. (As Kinsey *et al*. established in the 1953 work, only a negligible percentage of sexual acts is motivated by the desire for offspring.) It should be noted, however, that there have been a number of dissenting views. For example, Van de Velde has asserted that "to be a woman means to have the desire to become a mother both physically and mentally...The absence of the maternal instinct in the modern woman is really nothing but a pose .... A more than temporary repression of the mother instinct is, practically speaking, impossible."

The other aspect of the so-called maternal instinct, i.e., the post-maternal, fares little better when subjected to analysis in terms of the three criteria. Although it is true that instances of maternal devotion are widespread throughout the animal kingdom, numerous exceptions exist. And even when the behavior does take place, the explanation does not have to be in terms of a genetically determined mother-young bond. In one of the standard texts on instinct, by Tinbergen, a total of nine different examples of allegedly instinctive post-maternal behavior are described, each of which can be alternatively interpreted to be the result of stimulus-response sequences in which maternal solicitude plays no role. A representative case is the feeding behavior that pigeons display toward their young. The regurgitative method of feeding that is employed can be readily explained as follows:[10] hormonal changes cause the engorgement of the crop (a pouch-like portion of the gullet), making it sensitive to emetic stimuli provided by the movements of the squab's head against the breast. The regurgitative reaction has been described by one writer, Levi, as displaying "the utmost gentleness and tenderness." It seems more likely, however, that it should be regarded, in Whitman's words, "not as a special instinctive act... but rather as ordinary vomiting elicited under special conditions." The parent bird, reinforced by what has occurred, can be expected to keep coming back for more of the same kind of satisfaction. This pattern of behavior does keep the squab (and the species) alive, but the instinct involved—if, indeed, "instinct" is a useful concept here—

might better be called regurgitative than maternal. Any object (a finger, a toothbrush, a pencil) that provided the requisite stimulation would be rewarded with the same regurgitated goodies.

Turning to the organic-basis criterion, we find a complex set of variables implicated in post-maternal behavior. Not only are there hormones that increase the likelihood of such behavior, but also there are certain drives that can help to explain the mother's attachment to her young. Two of these are particularly important, not only in human mothers but in others mammals as well: the tendency to seek relief from the painful pressure of engorged mammary glands (roughly analogous to the hormonally induced crop-engorgement found in pigeons), and the desire or need for tactile stimulation. Stimulation of body surfaces must be, if we may judge from the face-rubbing, hair-patting, foot-tapping, and hand-holding that constitute such a large segment of our everyday activity, a quite important motive for most of us, and one requiring almost constant gratification. For many new mothers, the cuddling of the soft-skinned baby probably satisfies the motive more frequently and reliably than do the occasional embraces of the husband. And it is a truism that we develop positive feelings toward sources of satisfaction. As anthropologist Weston La Barre has put it, "the physiological gratification of the mother is behind the prodigies of care of her baby." This gratification, along with the aforementioned relief of mammary gland discomfort, may help to explain the fact that in those Australian tribes that practice infanticide, the baby is likely to be spared once it has been nursed by its mother.[11]

A rather weak argument is sometimes brought up at this point: there *is* a post-maternal instinct, some will say, because the nine months of carrying the unborn baby during pregnancy can be very satisfying ones for the mother, thus making a close emotional involvement virtually inevitable. But clearly such an attachment would be learned, rather than instinctive. Also, pregnancy is often a time (in our society) of considerable discomfort, so that many of the feelings a woman may develop for her unborn baby are quite different from love.

The widespread occurrence of infanticide is relevant when we examine the post-maternal instinct in terms of the criterion of universality. It is difficult—although, as we shall see, not quite impossible—to maintain that the post-maternal instinct exists when there are so many societies in which mothers kill their newborn babies. Of course, not every instance of infanticide provides evidence against the post-maternal instinct theory. Many anthropologists have reported the reluctance with which mothers kill their infants in response to dire economic necessities or unbreakable ritualistic requirements. But some of the reasons for infanticide seem not quite so compelling. Klineberg reports that the Murray Islanders engaged in the custom in order to equalize the number of boys and girls. In various parts of Melanesia, as Sumner & Keller point out, the following reasons were reportedly not unusual: vanity (i.e., avoidance of the malformations of the breast believed to result from nursing), vengeance (i.e., a way of getting even with the child's father, for a presumed insult), and discipline (if a child becomes too demanding, "its parents do not indefinitely tolerate the annoyance"). Mead reported in 1949 that certain women in Natchez Indian society would strangle their children with their own hands in order to attain a higher social status, and Briffault's *The Mothers* mentions that the Abipones of the Gran Chaco never permitted more than two of their children to survive;

all others were killed to "save trouble." The flimsy nature of this alleged instinct is well illustrated by the case, cited by Miller, of the Californian Indians whose infanticide rate was greatly reduced when missionaries started giving maternity bonuses. But perhaps it is Thomas who describes the most extreme example of non-maternal behavior, involving the Tahitian Ariori, who were required to kill all their children at birth.[12]

Infanticide is not the only kind of occurrence that casts doubt on the existence of a post-maternal instinct at the human level. For example, Sumner reports that the Ngumba offered their offspring in payment of debts and fines, and that Gilbert Islanders would permit a newborn to be adopted by its grandparents, to compensate for the mother's leaving home. (As will be remembered, pregnancy was welcomed by the Gilbert Islanders as a culturally acceptable excuse for leaving the home of the maternal grandparents. See p. 61.)

The emphasis in the foregoing examples has been on behavior, rather than on the emotional responses of the mothers. This emphasis is unavoidable, because very few of the anthropological reports allude to maternal feelings in these cases. Briffault reports, however, in *The Mothers*, that Dayak mothers "part with their babies apparently without a pang," and that Aleut parents "were always willing to give up their children to any relatives or even to strangers, to be brought up."

To summarize, it may be said that there are many societies in which maternal drives, whether pre- or post-, seem to be either nonexistent or of very slight intensity; and that where a strong maternal drive *can* be found, it is probably learned rather than instinctive. There is certainly no evidence that all "normal" women desire to have children. Or, expressed somewhat more vigorously, "Women don't need to be mothers any more than they need, in an Italian restaurant, to order spaghetti."[13] And it has already been established that there is nothing necessarily wrong with a man who neglects to beget. We may conclude, with Kenkel, that "a married couple that never goes through the child-bearing stage does not for this reason constitute an unhealthy, stunted, or pathologically abnormal family."[14]

Undeniably, many men and women express the desire for an opportunity to guide, help, and nurture young people. When these commendable desires are accompanied by the necessary child-rearing skills, we have the makings of a nuclear family at its best. Unfortunately, many of the people who express these sentiments are merely parroting the social phrases that have been conditioned into them, thus concealing (perhaps from themselves as well as others) the less lofty motives that are actually operating. Also, even the loftiest of pre-parental intentions may crumble in response to the pressures of parenthood. And finally, even the best of nuclear families may be less conducive to human growth than are other child-rearing settings (see Chapters V and VI).

In a society that does not stigmatize illegitimacy, men and women would not have to get married in order to satisfy whatever pre- or post-parental drives they might have. The desire for children may be a very real reason for marrying in our society, but it certainly cannot be regarded as a justification for the institution of marriage. (The possibility of mother and child being deserted constitutes a separate problem and will be dealt with later.)

Murdock, in 1949, concisely summarized the conventional functions of the family, as we know it: "In the nuclear family or its constituent relationships we thus see assembled four functions fundamental to human social life—the sexual, economic, reproductive, and educational."[15] The first three of these have now been discussed, and we may accordingly turn to an examination of the fourth. By "education," Murdock refers broadly to socialization and to the type of upbringing necessary for proper physical, emotional, and intellectual development. The question then becomes, Do children need parents?

IV

Are Parents Necessary?

PEOPLE IN ALL WALKS of life, of all degrees of intelligence, and with all shades of philosophical, religious, and political persuasion, are usually able to agree on one subject: mother. Motherhood in general, and mothers in particular, are revered, respected, virtually deified, and anyone who attacks "Mom" is likely to be regarded as a crackpot, a communist, or a kid who will eventually outgrow his rebelliousness.

And yet, there is no scientific evidence to support the assertion that children "need" either of their parents. Of course the young child, because of his relative helplessness, does need adult caretakers, but the suggestion will be made in this chapter that the caretakers in a child-care institution can do at least as good a job of bringing up a child as can his own parents.

The material that follows is taken from three sources: studies of institutionalized children, experimental studies of parentally-deprived animals, and anthropological accounts of parent-child separation. Most of the evidence in this chapter has been presented in greater detail in the 1961 and 1968 studies by the present author, and the interested reader is advised to refer to these earlier publications.

There are a number of child-care institutions in the United States and abroad that are undeniably (although often avoidably) responsible for grave and long-lasting damage to their young residents. Inadequate diet, untrained personnel, etc., produce hazards that are, fortunately, being eradicated through the efforts of alert and knowledgeable agencies and professional specialists. But the claim is still frequently made that institutionalization will *inevitably* result in serious physical, emotional, and intellectual ill effects, some of which may be irreversible. Many writers have also alleged that these ill effects can be relieved, if at all, only by reuniting the child with its mother or by providing it with a single mother-substitute (as contrasted with the multiple, relatively impersonal institutional caretakers). It is true that children in most institutions, even in those that seem to provide at least adequate physical care, frequently do display alarming symptoms of retardation or pathology. These symptoms have led a number of psychologists and others to maintain that every child needs, above and beyond the obvious physiological satisfactions, the particular kind of attention that is called "mothering" or "tender, loving care." But these terms are almost never defined, nor are their components very often regarded as worthwhile subjects of inquiry.

It is possible that the concept of "mother love" is so readily and uncritically embraced because it is so congenial to current cultural norms and to our real or imagined early life experiences. But no matter how comforting the concept may be, and no matter how much "common sense" it may seem to embody, it still requires scientific investigation and specification. (One may note, in passing, that "father love" is regarded by most authorities as being far less important, at least during the early years of life.)

The studies that have allegedly demonstrated the child's need for a mother are not, I believe, either conclusive or persuasive, because they fail to take into account a number of crucial factors. The first of these concerns the age at which the separation from the mother occurred. Since ill effects may result not from the maternal deprivation itself, but rather from the rupture of an already existing emotional bond with the mother, only those separations beginning before the establishment of this bond can furnish data concerning the effects of deprivation *per se*. Evidence from many quarters suggests that this bond is not definitely established until about the age of six months. This being the case, we would expect to find few if any serious emotional reactions to separation from the mother when this occurs during the first half-year of life. This expectation has been confirmed by a large number of studies.[1]

The fact that ill effects may follow maternal separation *after* the age of six months cannot be regarded as evidence that children need the loving care of their mothers, but only that they need whatever interpersonal relationship they may have become dependent upon. Indeed, the negative consequences of these post-six-month separations may be viewed as an argument against parental upbringing of children: if the emotional bond is never formed, the child is protected from the ill effects of deprivation. Supporting this position, Robertson, in 1953, revealed that those children who had not enjoyed a close relationship with their mothers appeared to be unperturbed when separated from their mothers at ages ranging from eighteen to twenty-four months. In another study, by DiBartolo & Vinacke, preschool children who had previously experienced a high degree of nurturance showed signs of behavioral deterioration when they were deprived of nurturance; there were no such signs among the "low-nurturance" children. These "withdrawal symptoms" do not, as some might maintain, constitute evidence that all children need love, any more than "withdrawal symptoms" from heroin mean that all people need drugs. Both types of dependence are learned; neither is inevitable, and neither is necessarily desirable.

Age at separation is not the only important variable in analyzing the effects of institutionalization; also significant is the nature of the children who are institutionalized. Most of the dire reports seem to imply that the children would have developed perfectly normally if they had remained at home. But it must be remembered that institutionalized children are usually atypical; they are likely to have a less favorable heredity and less favorable early environment than "normal" children. Bodman reported that more than 70% of a sample of institutionalized children had relatives known to be emotionally unstable, and that this factor fully accounted for the observed social immaturity. In Western society, early separation from parents is a rare occurrence, reflecting special circumstances. Was the child already ill? Were his parents unable, because of financial, medical, or psychological difficulties, to care for it? Had he been an unwanted baby? We know, from the study by Nilsson, Kaij & Jacobson, that women who have babies they don't want are relatively more susceptible to post-partum mental disorders. If the child lived at home before being institutionalized, it may have suffered because of its mother's mental condition. (This is still another reason to be cautious when interpreting the effects of separations beginning after the age of six months.) The possibility also exists that there are institutionalized children with serious congenital defects that escape early clinical diagnosis.[2] Thus, the frequent statement that symptom severity is directly related to duration of institutionalization may be misleading.

Another reason not to accept this correlation between length of separation and severity of ill effects is that it is unsound to compare a group of children who have been institutionalized for, say, two years with another group who have been institutionalized for only three or four months. A selective factor may be operating. Since most child-care institutions also serve as adoption agencies (or as adjuncts thereof), most of their residents will eventually be adopted. The more attractive and responsive children are the most likely to be selected, so that those who remain, as Stott pointed out in 1957, do not constitute a fair sample of the institutional population but probably include a disproportionate number of children who are below average in potential. Such children are not only less likely to be selected by the prospective adoptive parents but are also less likely to be offered for adoption, because, according to Simon & Bass, many adoption agencies commonly retain in institutions or foster homes those children judged to be below average.

It is also true that the children whose defects allegedly spring from institutionalization have had, in general, unfavorable pre-natal environments. For example, a relatively large number of institutionalized children are the offspring of women from lower socio-economic classes, and such women are especially likely to suffer from dietary deficiencies. Montagu gave statistics, in 1950, showing that the children of women malnourished during pregnancy have incidence rates for bronchitis, pneumonia, rickets, tetany, dystrophy, and anemia that are 2½ times higher than do children with better pre-natal environments; and the incidence of premature births is more than four times greater.

Inadequate nutrition during the gestation period is not the only cause of unfavorable pre-natal environment. Anxiety and other unpleasant emotions during pregnancy are known to have serious consequences on the offspring, including the possibility of mental deficiency (Stott, 1962), and schizophrenia (Oltman & Friedman). Norris found that the unwed status of many of the mothers of institutionalized children may well lead to biochemical stress and fetal damage of varying degrees of severity; and, according to Wortis, illegitimacy also is correlated with a relatively high incidence of prematurity. Beskow's results indicate that the two conditions appear to have a cumulatively negative effect. Indeed, any unwanted pregnancy has a good chance of being a difficult, dangerous one; and it is safe to say that a very large proportion of institutionalized children result from unwanted pregnancies. Is it reasonable to place the blame for all their deficiencies on their institutionalization?

The dangers of prematurity are particularly noteworthy, because of evidence from many sources that there is a higher proportion of prematurely born infants in institutions than would be expected by chance (see, for example, Weidemann's 1959 article). Montagu found, in 1950, that children born prematurely are relatively more likely to be retarded in language and muscular development and coordination, their attention span is likely to be shorter, they tend to be shy and highly emotional, and they more frequently have feeding difficulties and other behavior disorders than do children born at full term.[3] Zitrin, Ferber & Cohen have also found prematurity to be statistically related to schizophrenia; Sarvis & Garcia relate it to autism; Reardon, Wilson & Graham have found links between prematurity and increased susceptibility to infection and other stresses. All of the foregoing conditions have frequently been attributed to insufficient maternal love. Of particular interest, in view of the comments made previously concerning delayed effects, is the fact, as Tyson points out, that the premature child may seem quite healthy at first, so that later disabilities may be misinterpreted.

Still another cause of doubt concerning the claims that maternal deprivation causes malfunctioning is that institutionalized infants are frequently separated, according to Anna Freud, "not only from their mothers but from their home background...the other parent, possible siblings, all other inanimate familiar objects, sights, sounds, etc." Such a sudden and massive environmental shift, according to Gerwirtz's 1961 paper, may render the infant's usual repertoire of responses inadequate, leading to behavioral deterioration.

If recent research findings are confirmed, the variable of breast feeding will also have to be taken into account. Institutionalized babies are less likely to have been breast-fed before being separated from their mothers; as Turner points out, "Clinicians are aware that worry, fear, embarrassment, sadness, and other strong emotions at the time of nursing may inhibit the flow of milk in women." And, of course, there is little likelihood of breast-feeding after institutionalization. If it is true, as suggested by György, Dhanamitta & Steers, that human milk has immunological qualities not found in cow's milk or in standard formulas,[4] the lowered resistance of institutionalized infants to infection could be readily explained without recourse to the love-deprivation theory. Bakwin's 1964 conclusion that eczema, tetany, and respiratory illnesses are found more frequently in artificially fed babies is also worthy of note. And in view of the previously mentioned high proportion of prematures in most institutional populations, it is significant that (a) most premature babies are not breast-fed, and (b) prematures who are not breast-fed have the highest rates of morbidity and mortality. Absence of breast-feeding may also serve to reduce the amount of tactile stimulation received by the child. The importance of this variable will be discussed in detail in later pages.

The importance of infection has been frequently overlooked in studies of institutionalized babies. But we know from Rothman's work that "listlessness, emaciation and pallor, relative immobility, quietness, unresponsiveness to stimuli, indifferent appetite, failure to gain weight, poor sleep, an appearance of unhappiness, proneness to febrile episodes, and absence of sucking habits" may all result from respiratory infections or diarrhea contracted in the institution; when the last two other ailments have been successfully treated, the symptoms often disappear. Once again, mother-love appears to be an unnecessary variable.

Many studies of institutionalized children include observations made after the children have been placed in foster homes. Indeed, Schwartz finds that one-half of all illegitimate babies in the United States spend some part of their lives in foster homes. But Glaser, in 1962, has indicated that many individuals become foster parents solely for the financial reward or for reasons suggesting psychopathology. Such caretakers would certainly not be conducive to normal psychological development. Nor would the large number of shifts in foster homes that so often befall the maternally deprived child be likely to permit the stable milieu that may be necessary for the establishment of psychological stability. Also, Babcock proposes that the lower-class environments provided by so many foster parents may be relatively inefficient in promoting the development of the young child.[5] And still another possibly harmful factor, mentioned by Tezner, is the emotional triangle that sometimes develops between foster mother, biological mother, and child. In short, we should not be surprised by the findings of Maas & Engler that about half of the children living in foster homes suffer from severe emotional difficulties.

Related to the foregoing considerations is the fact that children who are not living with their own parents are frequently made to feel different from their peers. In particular, their illegitimacy makes them fair game for ridicule and ostracism that may leave lifelong scars.

But despite all these reasons for caution, and despite the fact that so many institutionalized babies suffer such extreme perceptual and social deprivation that explanation of malfunctioning in terms of deprivation of love becomes superfluous (see p. 92, ff.), a number of psychologists and psychiatrists persist in preferring the latter explanation. For example, a very influential 1951 survey by the British psychoanalyst John Bowlby cites 45 studies in support of his view that maternal deprivation does have serious deleterious effects. Individually and collectively, these studies have done much to create the present climate of opinion regarding the dire consequences of such deprivation. Bowlby's monograph has even been called, in Alpert's words, "the new Bible." But 33 of the 45 studies can be discounted at once, either because separation from the mother occurred after the age of six months, or because the institution involved was neither named nor described. And the present author has shown, in 1961, the twelve remaining reports cited by Bowlby to be unacceptable as evidence in support of the maternal deprivation hypothesis. Furthermore, it is interesting to note that in at least three of these reports, the authors make statements strikingly at variance with the position they are allegedly supporting. Thus, Bakwin reported in 1949 that, on a visit to "a large foundling hospital which houses some 250 children, more than half of whom are under one year of age," he was unable to find "a single baby who showed the clinical features which have come to be associated with emotional deprivation in young infants." He attributes this low level of pathology to the large amount of stimulation received by the children. But, it should be remembered, the stimulation was non-maternal. In Bowlby's presentation of Bakwin's work, reference is made to a few case studies that might lend themselves to the maternal deprivation hypothesis, but there is no mention of the 250 children who appeared to be symptom-free. Similarly, while Bowlby cites an early study by Durfee & Wolf, 1933, he ignores what is perhaps the authors' most important conclusion: that the ill effects of institutionalization are not inevitable but can be averted by alert and intelligent administrators. And why, in his discussion of the 1944 findings of Anna Freud & Burlingham, did Bowlby neglect the statement that "babies between birth and about five months of age, when not breast-fed under either condition, develop better in our nursery than in the average proletarian household"?

By far the most influential publications cited by Bowlby are Ribble's 1943 study and Spitz's 1945(b) work, and we may regard these as typical examples of Bowlby's sources. It is rather surprising that these studies are still referred to with such frequency by other investigators and by textbook authors, since there is now ample evidence that they are, to put it mildly, inconclusive. Pinneau, who has presented in 1950 and 1955 the most detailed and impressive accounts of the many shortcomings of these studies, concludes—on the basis of statistical, methodological, and theoretical considerations—that neither Ribble nor Spitz has provided scientifically acceptable evidence that maternal deprivation has negative consequences.

Even if Pinneau's criticisms represented the point of view of one isolated psychologist, his arguments are sufficiently cogent to merit the most careful study. But his is no voice in the wilderness. Statements which cast doubt on the methods, findings, and/or conclusions of Ribble, Spitz, and others with similar views, occur with increasing frequency in the professional literature. For example, according to Anderson, "So extreme are [Ribble's] statements that almost every review in scientific journals has pointed out many misinterpretations of established fact." And in a well-known paper by Orlansky, we read, "It should be noted that in the cases of anaclitic depression reported by Spitz the children affected had each been accustomed since birth to the care and attention of their mothers. One wonders if the same reaction would have occurred had they not been accustomed to such personal attention during their first half year of life." It should be noted, in this connection, that the average age at which the children studied by Spitz were separated from their mothers was less than six months, so that only about half of them satisfied our age criterion.

But perhaps the most significant statement is C. W. Eriksen's 1957 comment on the Pinneau critique, and on Spitz's 1955 rebuttal: "Pinneau raises questions and points out defects in design, methodology, and statistics that would seem to leave Spitz's conclusions, at best, only suggestive. . . .Spitz, in this reviewer's opinion, fails adequately to meet the questions that have been raised. While most of us will continue to believe in the importance of mothering during infancy, we must recognize that this belief has more the characteristics of a faith and less the basis of demonstrated fact." This commendably frank acknowledgment, in the last sentence, raises many questions, but it also serves as a partial answer to the question of why the studies cited by Bowlby have gained such widespread acceptance among psychologists. The answer seems to reside less in the studies themselves than in the needs of psychologists.

In evaluating Bowlby's collection of studies, one author, O'Connor, concluded, "On the basis of...theoretical objections and on the basis of the evidence either offered or ignored, it must be said that Bowlby's thesis is not established....Its lack of exact logic in theory and the conflicting evidence on which it is based prevent this author from accepting the theory as it stands." Indeed, Bowlby himself has acknowledged that "some of the workers who first drew attention to the dangers of maternal deprivation resulting from separation have tended on occasion to overstate their case."[6]

Still, the fact that none of Bowlby's references offers satisfactory evidence that maternal deprivation is harmful does not mean that *all* studies in this field can be automatically dismissed. It may be instructive to consider some representative publications that have appeared subsequent to Bowlby's compilation.

A number of these make favorable mention of the reports of Spitz and others already cited, and then proceed to fall into some of the same errors that have been described above. (See the previously cited summaries by the present author.) Indeed, there is *no* persuasive evidence that deprivation of love is the most likely explanation of the ill effects of institutionalization. One might still argue that although not one of these reports can, alone, be regarded as conclusive, the fact that they all point in the same direction lends them some sort of credibility. This position is weakened, however, by the fact that there are a number of authors who not only fail to support the maternal deprivation hypothesis but also suggest, either directly or indirectly, that the hypothesis is incorrect. (It should be observed, however, that some of their interpretations are of a subjective nature and cannot be regarded as definitive evidence.) The following list is by no means complete,[7] but may be sufficient to serve as a counterbalance to the more publicized studies that seem to point in the other direction.

(1) Rheingold found, in 1956, that the mean intelligence score of the institutionalized babies she studied was within the normal range. A follow-up study, by Rheingold & Bayley, revealed that the group as a whole was friendly, of normal intelligence, and apparently well adjusted. "They did not resemble the emotionally disturbed and mentally retarded children described in studies of the effects of institutional life or separation from the mother." The same investigator, working with another group of children in 1961, found them to be interested, competent, and even more sociable than the family-reared infants who served as controls. She offers the following partial explanation for this finding: "Different caretakers, with their different appearances, voices, and manners of administering care, must provide a kind of stimulation the home infant would lack in the usual routine of his day."[8]

(2) Although Leon Yarrow, one of the leading students of the effects of maternal deprivation, has expressed the opinion that children need individualized attention, he reports research indicating no relationship between "exclusiveness of mothering" and any of the aspects of infant behavior that he studied.

(3) Banham failed to find ill effects in "the great majority" of the hundreds of institutionalized children she observed.

(4) Klackenberg has reported that "the results of

care in Stockholm infants' homes are very different from those described by Spitz."

(5) Heston, Denny, and Pauly found no difference in personality or intelligence between the control group and a group of adults who had been institutionalized for varying periods beginning at birth.

(6) The frequently encountered allegation that maternal deprivation predisposes the individual to criminality has been challenged by Naess, on the basis of contrary findings.[9]

(7) Case studies can seldom be conclusive, but a publication by Rose & Sonis at least indicates that not all case studies support Bowlby's conclusion. Gastrointestinal symptoms in two infants, aged three months and four months, disappeared shortly after, and apparently as a result of, institutionalization. As the authors conclude, "Structured and realistic separations are not inevitably traumatic."

(8) Spitz himself, in 1954, describes a case in which maternal deprivation was apparently beneficial. He also asserts that one fairly common cause of infant distress, the "three-month colic," is found relatively less often among maternally deprived infants.

(9) Schaffer found in 1965 that infants separated from their mothers before the age of six months suffered ill effects only when the institution was a grossly inadequate one. In a study published in the following year, he reported that "the extreme apathy described by Spitz was not characteristic of the present sample. This applied even to those infants who had spent the longest period [i.e., seven months] in hospital."

(10) Anna Freud and Sophie Dann present evidence that institutionalization may have definite advantages: "The feelings of the six children toward each other

show a warmth and spontaneity which is unheard of in ordinary relations between young contemporaries." Goldberger's follow-up study of these children (as cited by Jersild) revealed that their development was "as favorable as one might find if six children, chosen at random, were followed from early childhood into adult years."

(11) In three separate studies by the present author (1965a, 1965b, unpublished), the developmental level of infants residing in institutions was much higher than the adherents of the Bowlby-Spitz position would have led us to predict.

What can we conclude from the gradually accumulating body of data that has just been sampled? Occupying an intermediate position, one writer, Tezner, rejects the motto, "Better a bad family than a good institution," asserting that appropriate procedures can eliminate differences between institutionalized and family-reared children. But he appears to remain convinced of the need for love, replacing the aforementioned motto with a new one: "A good foster home is better than a good institution."

A more reasonable verdict, I believe, has been reached by other students of infant development. As one child psychologist, O'Connor, has put it, "Under some circumstances, life in an institution can be stimulating and improving." More specifically, Gewirtz commented in 1968 that "institutions can be engineered to provide relatively good environments for children, while a family setting may provide a relatively poor caretaking environment."[10] There can be no denying that most institutions, as they are currently set up, fail to meet the needs of their infant residents. But this is far from saying that the effects of institutionalization are inevitably deleterious. If certain changes—to be outlined below—were made, there is no reason to think that a relatively impersonal child-rearing environment need have any adverse consequences whatsoever.

If it is true that the emotional, intellectual, and physical deficits or decrements often found in institutionalized children cannot rightly be attributed to absence of maternal love, the question remains as to why institutionalization so frequently *is* followed by ill effects. Some possible answers in terms of age at separation, likelihood of non-random sampling, etc. have already been mentioned. We now turn to what is, in this writer's opinion, the most important variable of all: the nature of the post-separation environment.

The Perceptual Deprivation Hypothesis

Human infants, like infants in all the other species we know anything about, must receive adequate stimulation of their various senses if they are to develop properly. Furthermore, this stimulation should be provided on a regular basis, permitting the establishment of associations among stimuli and between particular stimuli and particular responses. Although institutions *can* provide adequate sensory and perceptual[11] stimulation, most of them do not—not so much from understaffing, as from insufficient understanding of infants' needs. The reader should note, while reading the following survey of the available evidence, that *all* of the reported deficiencies in stimulation can be easily remedied within existing institutional settings.

It has been pointed out by this author in his monograph on tactile stimulation, and by Rheingold in 1960, that institutionalized infants generally do not receive as much tactile stimulation as do family-reared infants. L.

K. Frank, one of the first to note the possible dangers of insufficient skin contact, warned in 1957 that it "may establish in the baby persistent emotional. . .responses to the world, since his initial biological reactions to threats have not been allayed and hence may become chronic." For Frank, tactile stimulation (the need for which, he believes, may be learned in the womb) is largely responsible for the individual's eventual verbal abilities and for all of the baby's perceptions and interactions in the outside world.[12]

Another commentator, Ashley Montagu, asserted in 1953 that "tactile stimulation during infancy, and especially during the first months of nursing, is extremely important for the subsequent development of the person. . . .On the physical level, it may be suggested that persons who have received insufficient tactile stimulation in infancy are frequently shallow breathers. . .more susceptible to disorders of the gastro-intestinal and respiratory tracts and possibly the genito-urinary tract."

Psychoanalytically oriented writers, who generally stress the importance of maternal affection, have also acknowledged the considerable role played by physical contact. Spitz reported in 1954 that children whose mothers did not like to touch them were especially likely to develop dermatitis, to have inadequate social relations and memory defects, and to suffer deficiencies in locomotor behavior. Anna Freud (as cited by Spitz in 1957) also regarded lack of skin contact as an important cause of later disturbances.

There is not yet a very large body of experimental evidence to support the clinically derived impression that tactile stimulation is of major developmental significance. But a study of tactile stimulation by the present author, although on a relatively small scale, may serve as a useful model for more extensive work. Using institutionalized babies as subjects, I provided half the group with twenty minutes per day of extra handling. The handling was done in a purely mechanical way, and the research assistants who served as handlers were trained to avoid any display of affection or tenderness. At the end of ten weeks, the children who had received this extra tactile stimulation showed statistically significant gains in development when compared to the control group that had received only the amount of stimulation normally available in the institution. Also of interest is the finding of White & Held that babies who are handled show greater visual attentiveness than those who are not.[13] This finding is especially significant in view of the fact that most of the tests that measure psychological development early in life involve visual or visual-motor skills (e.g., reaching for a dangling ring).

Research with lower animals has confirmed the major role played by skin stimulation. In a well-known series of experiments, Harlow and his associates studied the behavior of rhesus monkeys reared by "substitute mothers"—objects made of cloth or wire and designed to provide nourishment by means of bottles lodged in the "chest." The monkeys showed considerable attachment to the cloth substitutes, and Harlow concluded that "the security that the infant...gains from the presence of the real mother is no greater than the security it gains from a cloth surrogate."[14] The same investigator found, in 1961, that infant monkeys that had been deprived of sufficient skin contact would invariably exhibit profound distress, characterized by crying, rigid immobility, or the peculiar type of convulsive, rocking, jerking motion so frequently encountered among neglected or brain-damaged human children.[15] Research by Beckett *et al.* has revealed that the same sort of abnormal blood chemistry is found in tactilely deprived rhesus monkeys as is found in human schizophrenic patients.

It is reasonable to suggest, therefore, that some of the ill effects alleged to stem from maternal deprivation are actually the consequences of insufficient tactile stimulation. In fact, Temerlin and his associates, the authors of one study involving treatment of a group of retarded children, asserted that "the failure to find any evidence of a differential effect of mothering and skin contact ...probably means that future investigators can safely treat them as a single independent variable."

But there are other forms of stimulation also likely to be deficient in many institutions. Institutionalized babies are not picked up as frequently as family-reared infants, according to Rheingold's 1960 study, and thus suffer a reduction in the type of stimulation that affects the vestibular apparatus of the inner ear.[16] The beneficial effects of motion on infants, well known to Plato (*Laws*, Book 4) have been rediscovered in recent years. Bender has asserted that self-awareness, as well as awareness of the outside world, originates in sensations of up-down movement. Racamier points out that depriving a child of mobility reduces his opportunities for normal social relations. A child-carrying procedure found in some parts of Japan, which involves providing the young child with a very high level of vestibular stimulation, has been described by Moloney as a "vaccination against psychosis." Recent experiments by Korner & Thoman indicate that picking up and holding the baby in an upright position is even more effective than simple tactile stimulation in promoting alertness.[17] Also, Launay and associates have established a link between prolonged immobility and rhino-pharyngeal infection; and Friedman, Handford & Settlage relate immobility to inappropriate responses to pain and to aggressiveness and abnormal activity levels later in life. In a series of articles for nurses, Olson and associates list the following "hazards of immobility": colic-like pain, nausea, vomiting, tracheitis, bronchitis, pneumonia, reduction in bone calcium, atrophy of muscle tissue, ulcerated skin, hormonal malfunctioning, cardiac failure, and respiratory failure.[18] Also, Schaffer, in 1966, presented evidence that babies deprived of adequate movement are particularly vulnerable to other forms of deprivation. Finally, as Gesell pointed out in 1946, it is probable that premature babies, so frequently found in institutions, are especially likely to suffer from this kind of deprivation because of their early confinement to incubators and similar containers. It should not be surprising, therefore, that Neal has found supplementary vestibular stimulation to have a positive influence on the development of premature infants.

We cannot, of course, conduct experiments in which infants are intentionally deprived of opportunities for movement. But there is no reason to suppose that "the profound metabolic changes occurring in persons confined to bed rest," as found by Bakwin & Bakwin, do not also afflict the babies studied by Spitz (1945a), who could not move freely because of the deep hollows that had formed in their mattresses.

A number of relevant studies involving sub-human primates have been described by Mason, Davenport & Menzel. These authors cite evidence that movement-deprived chimpanzees are likely to engage in excessive rocking behavior. It is precisely this sort of behavior, when encountered in institutions, that is usually attributed to deprivation of love.

As might be expected, more than one type of stimulation may be necessary if a particular type of normal behavior is to appear on schedule. Multiple sensory or perceptual deprivation may thus have consequences beyond those associated with each modality considered separately. A good illustration of the effects of such a combined deficit can be found in Fischer's study of a group of three-month-old institutionalized infants, more than a quarter of whom failed a developmental test item that is almost never failed by family-reared infants of that age level. In the words of the investigator, "the behavior in question [small fraction of weight carried briefly, held standing], a forerunner of later standing and walking behavior, may be influenced by child-rearing differences, most probably by specific tactile stimulation and amount of experience in being moved about in a pleasurable way."

Movement and skin stimulation are by no means the only forms of experience of which institutionalized infants are likely to be deprived. Dennis & Najarian described in 1957 an institution in which the children's scores on the Cattell Infant Scale (one of the better-known developmental tests) were quite low. But the interpretation of the authors goes far deeper than the usual automatic reference to maternal deprivation. One especially noteworthy departure is that the examining instrument is itself examined: "Beyond the two-months level the majority of items on the Cattell Scale require that the infant be tested in a sitting position while being held on the lap of an adult," and the inmates of this particular institution had been quite unaccustomed to such luxury.[19] Indeed, the authors comment that for no item included in the test for this age range had the babies received adequate prior experience. In a 1960 publication, Dennis has suggested that the early deprivation of experience in the sitting or prone position may result in long delays in learning to walk, so that "the explanation of retardation as being due primarily to emotional factors is believed to be untenable." Experimental evidence in support of this position is now available. Sayegh & Dennis found that systematically giving babies experience in sitting and in manipulating objects resulted in sizable improvements in test performance. At a more basic level, we know from French's work that postural regulation requires the proper functioning of the reticular formation—a part of the nervous system whose activity requires adequate sensory stimulation (see page 109).

Of the many other sensory modalities that are under-stimulated in most institutional settings, vision is perhaps the most important. Drever's research with blind subjects indicates that visual deprivation is especially harmful when it begins early in life. And institutionalized babies *are* visually deprived, at least in those older institutions that provided so much of the data upon which the "mother love" theory depends. For hygienic reasons, it used to be (Goldfarb's 1955 study provides a representative example) standard practice to place the babies in cribs that were covered on all four sides by white sheets. And even the minimal stimulation provided by the sheets was short-lived: as Bexton, Heron & Scott point out, "When stimulation does not change, it rapidly loses its power to cause the arousal reaction." The poor performance of institutionalized children on developmental tests, with their preponderance of items requiring visual skills, should occasion no surprise, especially when we realize that adequate visual experience has been found necessary for the normal development of the optic system (see Langworthy's 1933 article).[20] Moreover, Goldstein has established that it is not so much the stimulus itself as the *response* to the stimulus that provides the needed perceptual stimulation, and that this responsiveness should be exercised in infancy if reactivity is to develop normally. The baby immobilized in the deep hollows of a mattress is unlikely to be very responsive to visual or any other kind of stimulation.

Experimentation with lower animals gives added credence to these conclusions. For example, Wilson & Riesen found that monkeys reared with a minimum of visual experience may suffer long-term visual defects, sometimes involving deterioration of the optic tract. And opportunities for the exploration of the immediate environment have been found to be necessary for normal development in many other species (see Christie's survey of the research literature). How much exploring can a human infant do if he is confined to his crib for nearly 24 hours every day? In a fine example of understatement, Spitz has conceded, in his study with Wolf, that such restriction "probably has a certain influence in the sphere of intellectual development." Frequent and regular out-of-crib experiences might go far toward alleviating the allegedly inevitable consequences of institutionalization.

Perhaps retardation in speech development is the most frequently encountered effect of institutionalization (aside from the emotional problems to be discussed later). Those language deficits that persist within an institutionalized population probably result, in large part, from inadequate exposure to language. Verbal stimulation during the "preverbal" months is of considerable importance. The average infant must be exposed to spoken language for about eight months before he can comprehend speech; and, as Myklebust points out, more advanced forms of language functioning, such as speaking and reading, require a firm foundation of more basic language skills.[21] If eight months of normal speech-reception are necessary for the development of comprehension, it is easy to see why institutionalized children, who are, as Rheingold found in her 1960 study, rarely spoken to during the early months of life, are slow to develop in this area. Other forms of early deprivation may also contribute to language retardation. Insufficient auditory stimulation—apart from verbal stimulation—has, for example, been found by Eisen to be an important determinant. And, rather surprisingly, the present author discovered in 1965(a) that supplementary tactile stimulation was found to improve the early language functioning of a group of institutionalized infants.

Because so many of the senses receive insufficient stimulation within the walls of most institutions, it seems appropriate to ascribe the ill effects of institutionalization to perceptual (or sensory) deprivation. Such an explanation seems preferable to the more highly specific explanations in terms of specified modalities (tactile, visual, etc.), and is far more useful than the vague and unsupported maternal deprivation hypothesis.

Even Spitz has occasionally published comments favoring the perceptual deprivation hypothesis. For example, in 1945(a): "Experimental investigation has proved that the trauma suffered by infants in public welfare institutions was due to the lack of stimuli. This lack of stimuli made it impossible for a normally integrated perceptive organization to develop. Consequently, the adaptation of these infants to their environment was handicapped by inadequate sensory perception and equally inadequate motor responses." In 1950, he recommended increasing the amount of tactile, auditory, and visual stimulation available to institutionalized children. It should also be noted that Ribble acknowledged that the mother is an important source of "stimulus feeding," particularly tactile, auditory, and kinesthetic sensory experience.

If the ill effects encountered when maternal separation occurs during the first half-year of life can be attributed primarily to perceptual deprivation, while ill effects found after later separations are primarily the combined results of perceptual deprivation and the severing of a close emotional attachment, then we should expect to find differences in reactions to the two types of experiences. This expectation has been confirmed in Schaffer's 1958 study of infants who had been hospitalized at ages from three weeks to 51 weeks. "We find a very' different pattern before seven months from that occurring after this age.... The operative factor in the infant's experience in hospital is one that can best be described as *perceptual monotony*" [italics in original].

Other writers have come to similar conclusions, proposing, in the case of Brody, "the absence of sensory stimulation as the chief cause of the impoverishment in the emotional life of the hospitalized infant," and stressing, as do Glaser & Eisenberg, that "unrelenting efforts to provide optimally stimulating environments for deprived children are emphatically justified clinically."

The relationship between perceptual stimulation and the development of the mother-child relationship is made explicit in this formulation by Moss: "The experiencing of mild stimulation is as essential for the infant's well-being as is the reduction of intense stimulation... Since the mother provides most of the mild stimulation for the baby, a close tie (dependency), ... is established with the mother."[22]

A series of reports dealing with young Ugandan children, published by Geber in 1958 strikingly illustrates the importance of early perceptual stimulation. The typical seven-week-old Ugandan baby is able to support himself in a sitting position—a feat not accomplished by the average European or American child until the age of 20 weeks. Similarly, children in Uganda are able to walk to a testing box and look inside when only seven months old; the average Western child cannot do this until the age of 15 months. And a number of other such comparisons all indicate the apparent superiority of the Ugandan child. How can this precocity be explained? The answer seems to lie in the very high level of stimulation provided by the mother. "She never leaves him, carries him on her back—often in skin-to-skin contact—wherever she goes, sleeps with him, feeds him on demand at all hours of the day or night, forbids him nothing, and never chides him. . . .He is, moreover, continually being stimulated by seeing her at various occupations and hearing her interminable conversations. . . . He is also the center of interest for neighbors and visitors to whom he is offered, as a matter of course, as soon as the usual greetings have been exchanged. If, however, he shows the slightest sign of displeasure, he is at once taken back by his mother." The developmental superiority of these children is probably not the result of any hereditary advantage. Ugandan children who were being reared in the European manner, "passing most of their lives in their cots and fed at regular intervals. . .did not show similar precocity after the first month. . ."[23] Geber reported similar findings for other parts of Africa in 1958 (b) and 1962.

These findings are extremely interesting, but they are not entirely free of ambiguity. For one thing, there is the problem of self-selection. Geber was certainly not in a position to divide the African women into two groups and to assign them, randomly, to the native and the European child-rearing procedures. It is possible that those women who chose the European style differed from the other women in ways that could affect their children. Also, the African method of rearing involves so many different components (including emotional components) that we have no way of knowing which are essential for rapid early development and which are not. To solve these problems, the experimental method is necessary. Reference has already been made to my own efforts in this direction (p. 93). In related studies by other authors,[24] supplementary stimulation of various modalities was also found to accelerate behavioral maturation.

While systematic reductions in stimulation have never been experimentally investigated with babies as subjects (fortunately for the babies!), there have been a number of relevant studies involving college volunteers and other older subjects. Although Jackson & Pollard have indicated that their generalizability may be open to question, these experiments provide us with a set of findings that are closely related to what we already suspect about similar deprivations in infants.

Most of these studies are quite similar in design and outcome. Subjects, after passing a preliminary test to screen out those with psychological problems, experience a period of relative perceptual deprivation. Auditory and visual stimulation is greatly reduced and is rendered patternless. In many experiments, the arms and legs are placed in cardboard sleeves that minimize movement. Feeding and toileting are accomplished with a minimum of perceptual stimulation. Though such a set-up might be considered a fine opportunity for resting, sleeping, or thinking, and though the subjects are usually paid a sizable sum for every hour they remain in the situation, most of them demand to be released after only a few hours. Anxiety attacks, hallucinations, and decrements in reasoning ability are just a few of the reported reactions.[25] In some cases, as noted by Bressler and associates, these ill effects may persist for days after the termination of the experiment. The need for stimulation is so urgent that, according to Lilly, deficits lead to "many, if not all, of the symptoms of the mentally ill," and, in Rosenzweig's words, the "cardinal symptoms of schizophrenia." It should be remembered that schizophrenia is supposed, by some, to be a result of love-deprivation.[26]

Serious as these effects may be, they are probably mild in comparison with the effects of sensory reduction on institutionalized infants. A student volunteer, or a hospital patient, may react less strongly to such a situation because of the knowledge that it is temporary. Not only is this comforting knowledge inaccessible to the infants, but also infant perceptual deprivation occurs at a time of life when normal stimulation can be neither anticipated by imagination nor re-created by memory.

Some writers have argued that the important factor in these sensory isolation experiments is not sensory at all, but has to do with the concomitant social isolation involved in such procedures. However, Leiderman and associates, who examined this particular issue, concluded that "the presence of another person was not always sufficient to alleviate the symptoms. Additional sensory stimuli were necessary before the psychotic process could be reversed." Indeed, as Schaffer stated in 1963, "the need for social stimulation arises from the need for stimulation." As Solomon and associates conclude, "the stability of man's mental state is dependent on adequate perceptual contact with the outside world."

Once again, studies of lower animals prove highly corroborative. Mitchell and associates, and Sackett, have found that rhesus monkeys respond to isolation with repetitive movements, such as rocking, and show abnormal sexual and other responses in puberty, long after the isolation experience has ended,[27] and Riesen provides similar evidence concerning chimpanzees. The psychiatrist David Levy describes head-shaking, tics, and other stereotyped responses to confinement in hens, horses, polar bears, black bears, lions, tigers, foxes, wolves, ocelots, jaguars, and hyenas. He attributes this behavior to movement restraint, but so many other forms of deprivation are also involved that it may be preferable to relate the behavior to non-specific perceptual deprivation. This latter interpretation receives partial support from Levy's own very important observation that "orphanage children are quickly cured of stereotyped movements by supplying normal outlets of interest and play." In a study of isolated, confined, perceptually deprived dogs, Melzack & Scott concluded that "early perceptual experience determines, in part at least, (a) the emergence of overt responses such as avoidance to noxious stimulation, and (b) the actual capacity to perceive pain normally." Might it not be that the "apathy" encountered in so many institutionalized infants is similarly caused? And if the infants fail to respond overtly to pain, the attending caretakers may not identify pathological processes until they take on serious proportions.

Only a few animal studies have systematically examined the effects of maternal deprivation *per se*. One study, by McClelland, revealed that rats that had been stroked in a mechanical fashion with a wire brush reacted as favorably as did those that had been gently stroked and petted by the experimenter. Experiments of this type may be quite relevant to the human condition. As Thompson put it " 'Mothering' a newborn infant is rather like 'gentling' a young rat. It is difficult to suppose that it involves anything more than stimulation or energization."

Harlow's research with rhesus monkeys, referred to earlier, is sometimes cited as evidence that mother-love is a prerequisite for normal development. (One may note, in passing, the tendency to reject evidence from lower animals if it does not support one's preconceptions. A finding that monkeys do not need love is likely to be shrugged off—"Who cares about monkeys, anyway?"—whereas a finding that can be interpreted in the opposite direction is embraced almost as avidly as Harlow's monkeys embraced their cloth mother-substitutes.) It is true that most of Harlow's subjects failed, when they reached physiological maturity, to engage in normal sexual or parental behavior. But we need to remember that the young monkeys had been deprived not only of their mothers, but also of other young monkeys. Is it not possible that this early social deprivation, rather than deprivation of maternal affection, is what led to the negative consequences? Further research from Harlow's laboratory provides an affirmative answer. Harlow & Harlow found in 1962 that monkeys raised on cloth substitutes do not show the usual psychosexual defects if they are given just 20 minutes per day of play time with one another. They state in their 1962 article on social deprivation in monkeys that, "It seems possible—even likely—that the infant-mother affectional system is dispensable, whereas the infant-infant system is the *sine qua non* for later adjustment in all spheres of monkey life."[28]

It should be obvious from the foregoing that Harlow's data *do not* support the contention that maternal affection is a variable of importance for normal, healthy development. Likewise, in a 1963 study by Davenport & Menzel involving chimpanzees, we find the suggestion that whereas "maternal care is sufficient to prevent stereotyped behavior from appearing. . .it is conceivable that these stimulus characteristics might be provided by general environmental enrichment and that hence the mother *per se* is unnecessary."

Kaufman & Rosenblum put forth evidence that a particular type of monkey (the pigtail) will show signs of depression if maternal separation occurs during infancy, but the depression disappears after about a week. Pigtail monkeys typically live in social groups characterized by rather indiscriminate "mothering" of all young of the species, regardless of biological maternity. As Lehrman pointed out in 1972, these observations suggest that reactions to maternal separation might be quite mild in societies that eliminate the intense, individualized mother-child bond that is embodied in our nuclear family structure.

Reviewing a large number of studies of many different species, D. O. Hebb concludes as follows: "The observed results seem to mean not that the stimulus of another attentive organism (the mother) is necessary from the first, but that it may become necessary only as psychological *dependence* on the mother develops" [italics in original]. Or, as Bindra puts it, "you can bring up a dog normally without attachment to the mother, and . . . there may be ways of doing the same in the case of human children."

Some of the ill effects sometimes attributed to maternal deprivation among lower animals may be explicable, as is suggested by Cairns' research, in terms of the post-separation rejection of the young by the mother or by the flock as a whole. Liddell's oft-cited studies of deprivation in sheep can thus be readily understood. Rather similar are the studies of monkeys by Green & Gordon and Lemmon & Patterson in which the investigators appear to have failed to take post-separation environment adequately into account.

Many research reports have been summarized in these pages, and some sort of recapitulation may be in order: those who believe that mother love is necessary frequently attempt to support their position by referring to the negative consequences of impersonal institutional upbringing. But these consequences are neither so inevitable, so irreversible, nor so serious as is often alleged. In many cases, the low level of functioning should not be attributed to institutionalization at all, but rather to several selective factors that result in most institutionalized children having two strikes against them by the time their group-rearing experience begins. And those children who *are* still normal when they enter the institution may well suffer because of (a) insufficient social stimulation (with consequent retardation in language and other social skills) and (b) insufficient perceptual or sensory stimulation. Although most institutions also lack the emotional intimacy and warmth found in most family settings, there is no evidence that this particular lack has any negative consequences whatsoever.

Every form of perceptual stimulation that is likely to be deficient in institutions—auditory, visual, tactile, vestibular, kinesthetic—has been found to play an important role in normal development. It may be that early perceptual impoverishment causes the young child to be especially dependent on those limited stimuli that remain available, and that changes in these result in psychological stress (see Hunt & Otis's 1963 article). This sequence may help to explain the child's maladaptive responses to new stimuli (strangers, testing instruments, etc.) within the institutional environment. In support of this interpretation is the finding by Moss, Robson & Pedersen that increases in visual and auditory stimulation at the age of three months were associated with a reduction in fear toward strangers at the age of nine months.

In view of the findings from infant research, adult sensory deprivation experiments, and studies of infrahuman animals, we should not be surprised by the low intelligence test scores recorded for institutionalized children nor by the occasional occurrence of psychotic-type reactions. What may be somewhat less apparent is the fact that virtually all of the alleged ill effects of love-deprivation are explicable in terms of perceptual and/or social deprivation, without any reference to emotional determinants. Excessive rocking may be a response, as Walters & Parke suggest, to insufficient auditory or visual stimulation; excessive crying may stem from perceptual monotony (Illingworth) or from the increased sensitivity to pain that follows visual deprivation (Zubek, Frye & Aftanas); absence of smiling can be traced back to inadequate stimulation;[29] Kunst found that thumb-sucking decreases when infants are in "a more stimulating situation than being in bed";[30] Selye traces a large number of skin diseases, including dermatitis and eczema, to defective adrenal gland functioning; and the latter defect may arise, in turn, Bovard indicates, from a deficiency in sensory stimulation.[31]

Perhaps the most important inference that can be drawn from this collection of human and infra-human research is that the stimulation necessary for optimal development need not be combined with a warm interpersonal relationship. Love, although probably not harmful, is superfluous.

But how is it possible for impersonally administered stimulation to have such massive effects? A large part of the answer is now available, thanks to our increasing knowledge of the workings of a section of the brain stem called the reticular formation. We know, for example, that any kind of stimulation activates not only the appropriate part of the brain (visual cortex, auditory cortex, etc.) but also, via the reticular formation, the brain as a whole. This arousal action is believed to be what keeps the brain awake, thus making possible, as Samuels suggests, the processes of learning and thinking.[32] The various types of perceptual deprivation therefore have not only specific negative effects, but general negative effects as well—a physiologically based conclusion that closely matches the conclusion derived from behavioral observations.[33]

The reader may be willing to grant that adequate perceptual and social stimulation is sufficient to insure *physical* and *intellectual* growth, and that these stimuli can be provided perfectly adequately within child-care institutions if personnel and resources were to be re-allotted in the light of what is now known about the requirements of the growing organism. But there may still be reservations concerning what is needed for proper *emotional* development. Can a love-deprived child learn to love? Will not such a child be cold, emotionless, devoid of precisely those feelings that make life most meaningful? The argument is an old and familiar one. Aristotle felt that the communal upbringing proposed by Plato would not work, because, as quoted by Zimmerman, "if children did not love their families, they would not be attached to anyone." And Spitz, in 1954, made a similar assertion: "De nourrissons sans amour ils deviendront des adultes pleins de haine."[34] But has this popular contention any validity?

The first point worth mentioning is that there is no good evidence for the claim that deprivation of love leads to later emotional impoverishment. Aside from a few poorly controlled studies, each of which has been disconfirmed (see, for example, the papers by Lowrey and Naess), no author has presented documentation for this assertion. There can be little doubt that sizable numbers of men and women, maternally deprived in infancy, fall in love and sustain relationships as well as those who have been brought up in more normal early environments.

Second, Marro presented evidence that criminals are likely to have very young or very old parents. This fact, coupled with statistics offered by Weidemann indicating that a disproportionate number of institutionalized infants are the offspring of parents who are either relatively young or relatively old, provides a genetic or pre-natal environmental alternative to the assertion that anti-social personality is the result of love-deprivation.

Third, we need to assess the assumptions underlying the contention that maternal deprivation gives rise to the inability to love. Do we really learn what love is by interacting with our mothers during infancy? Let us hope not. For the kind of love possible between mother and infant is directly related to the helplessness of the infant. It is a love based on dependency, on unequal status, on the infant's perception of the mother as the omnipotent source of food, warmth, and stimulation. Admittedly, many men marry women who will mother them, and many women become attached to "sugar daddies." But such attachments are antithetical to most standards of mental health. No, the kind of love that most people want their children to be capable of is not learned at the mother's breast. It is, rather, most likely to spring from relationships involving equal status. An institutional setting appears to be particularly desirable for this purpose.[35] Recall the finding, reported earlier (p. 90), that the institutionalized children studied by Anna Freud developed relationships with one another that showed "a warmth and spontaneity which is unheard of in ordinary relations between young contemporaries." It should also be noted here that some proponents of this position are inconsistent in claiming that we learn to love through the experience of being mothered, while also claiming that love is an instinctive feeling that is present in all humans and does not need to be learned.[36]

In a previous chapter, the point was made that the

intense emotional attachment between the sexes, which we call love, may be vastly overvalued. The same observation applies to conventional notions of the mother-child bond. As Bindra said:

> If the child is brought up to make a close attachment to one mother you will get one type of result; if he is brought up to make attachments to a large number you will get another type of result, and neither is good or bad for mental health in itself. Whether it is good or bad would depend on the kind of society in which this person is going to live.

What many people seem to forget is that absence of tender, loving care is not synonymous with rejection. Saying that rejection is likely to be harmful to the child is not, as Baumrind's work suggests, the same as saying that the child needs love. There is still no evidence that a "loving" parent does a better job than an emotionally neutral caretaker. Adequate perceptual stimulation, exposure to language, and a reduction in the usual child-caretaker ratio—these are some of the necessities that must be provided before we can fairly test the proposition that institutionalization is intrinsically detrimental to human development.[37]

Studies in Other Societies

One further approach to the problem of maternal deprivation is available: the anthropological approach. There are several societies in which parent-child separation customarily occurs. These would seem to offer excellent natural laboratories for studying the effects of separation, because the children are not the atypical, "high-risk" sample that is so often the case in our society. However, the obstacles to reliable data-collection and interpretation are so great as to render this approach quite unsatisfactory, at least for the present. It will, therefore, be treated here only briefly.

There is not a single example, in any of the societies for which adequate ethnographic reports are available, of maternal deprivation having adverse consequences. But although this absence of observed ill effects is in agreement with the position underlying this chapter, it obviously cannot be regarded as affording substantial support. In the first place, very few of the field investigators were trained psychologists or psychiatrists, and it is possible that childhood disturbances were present which escaped their notice. Second, in no case was the investigator specifically interested in the effects of maternal deprivation, and such information may have been regarded as not important enough to warrant study and/or publication. Third, since the field of cross-cultural infant testing is still in its infancy, any data that might be obtained would be of doubtful validity. (This lack of cross-cultural validity is a serious problem in personality-testing at older age levels as well.) And finally, each society differs from every other in so many variables besides that of child-rearing methods that it would be extremely hazardous to assert that whatever deficiencies might be found in the children or adults in a particular society resulted solely (or even partly) from maternal deprivation—or, for that matter, from perceptual deprivation.

Still, one does find an occasional anthropologist interested in this problem. We are told quite specifically, for example, by Dai, that mother-child separation, which was for a long time prevalent in Northern China, was not among the major causes of mental disturbance. Similarly,

Schulze stated in 1890 that in the Aranda society, the children show no affection for their parents and sometimes leave home to roam with other children. And Schram found that Monguor boys quite readily left their families, as early as age five, in order to stay with other families better off than their own. Still, the reliability of anthropological field reports—especially the less recent ones—is not always beyond question, nor are the descriptions of the societies complete enough, in terms of socio-psychological data, to permit proper evaluation.

Similar objections also apply, unfortunately, to numerous "Utopian" experiments, both in this country and abroad, that frequently instituted mother-child separation as part of their reform systems. Again, few observers were trained to make physical or psychological assessments of the children involved (especially since the bulk of these experiments were conducted at a time when testing instruments did not yet exist). Too, most of the Utopian groups did not last long enough to make accurate appraisal possible. It should be stressed, however, that the relatively short lifespans of these societies cannot be construed as a reflection upon the social reforms practiced therein. In virtually every case, the failure was attributable to improper administration, inadequate screening of new members, or social, economic, or legal pressures imposed from the outside. For example, the Oneida community (see p. 155) was doing quite well until the enactment of a law directed specifically against it.[38] In no case would it be correct to claim that the policy of maternal separation was itself responsible for the downfall of any of these societies. (See Holloway's 1951 publication.)

One seemingly prime candidate for study is the kibbutz movement in Israel. Children are separated from their parents shortly after birth and are reared in communal nurseries. And there has been no lack of competent investigators, observing, measuring, and reporting. The trouble (for our purposes) is that the child visits, or is visited by, his parents for a few hours each day and all day Saturday. Spiro, a leading authority on the subject, is probably correct in asserting, in 1955, that the kibbutz child interacts with his mother at least as much as does the child raised at home. To the extent that life in these collectives is relevant to the present discussion, it sheds light only on the effects of what has been called "intermittent mothering"—the combination of maternal and non-maternal caretaking. The results of this combination are reported, in general, to be more than satisfactory. According to Rabin, Rorschach (inkblot) tests reveal greater emotional stability and maturity in kibbutz-reared children than in Israeli children not reared on kibbutzim. Another writer reports that kibbutz children seem self-reliant, with little evidence of serious emotional disturbance, and that those few emotional conflicts that *are* experienced by the children are usually the results of conflicts between the parents and the caretaking personnel.[39] Thus, it is possible that if total separation from the parents could be achieved, emotional difficulties in the children would be reduced even further. But it is improbable that total separation will ever take place. Indeed, the opposite tendency seems to be developing. Bowlby's monograph, the flaws of which have already been discussed, has, Alpert indicates, "induced a precipitate reaction formation among kibbutzim away from Children's Homes and toward family rearing."

It should be obvious from these few examples that the anthropological approach, by itself, cannot provide us with any definitive answers. What it *can* do is lend further credence to the point of view derived from other sources: that children can thrive without benefit of maternal love. And if, as Havelock Ellis and many others have maintained, "marriage centers in the child and has at the outset no reason for existence apart from the welfare of the offspring," then, we may ask, why must we have marriage?

A summary of the argument, thus far, may be helpful: whatever its origins may have been, the institution of marriage is no longer necessary for the optimal functioning of our society or of the individual members of our society; sexual, economic, emotional, and child-rearing requirements have been shown to be readily satisfiable outside the bonds of matrimony. (Allegiance to the child-rearing function has been particularly tenacious among students of marriage, thus necessitating a lengthier consideration of the weaknesses of this position than was appropriate for the other functions.)

But the claim that marriage is unnecessary is not the same as the claim that marriage is undesirable. A plea for the complete social acceptance of non-marital forms of relationships can be taken more seriously after evidence has been presented concerning the harmful effects of marriage. It is to this evidence that we now turn.

V

The Destructiveness of Marriage

"IT IS IMPOSSIBLE to estimate the sacrifice of individual development and happiness that has been made to the family form, but it has been considerable." If this statement, made by Reed in 1929, is at all accurate, then still another justification—perhaps the ultimate one—for marriage ceases to be persuasive. But it is no easy matter to learn whether or not a marriage is happy. Certainly, answers to the direct question, "Are you happily married?" cannot be totally reliable. For many people, "happiness" has become synonymous with "mental health," and he who admits to an unhappy marriage may feel he is labeling himself an emotional or sexual misfit.

Then, too, we must ask, "Happier than what?" The single state, for most people in our society older than twenty, is no bed of roses.[1] To be single frequently means to be judged "unattractive," "unsuccessful," or "different" by one's acquaintances. But the chief offenders are usually one's parents (see Chapter II), who bombard with pleas and threats until the final capitulation.

It is possible, therefore, that in a marriage-crazy society like ours, those who yield are happier than those who do not. Groves, one of the staunch defenders of marriage, conceded that "a great part of the consequences of the negative interpretation the social conventions have given the status of the unmarried is registered in neurotic experience, producing one of the most frequent and difficult adjustment problems that come to the psychiatrist. However much the individual may be helped by psychoanalysis . . . , the difficulty from which he suffers is social, registering the unintelligent and even brutal methods of society in its attempt to maintain marriage adjustment as the norm of human association." Groves spells out the nature of this maladjustment. Marriage, he writes, "denies to a considerable number of men and more women all opportunity to achieve a socially approved and satisfying means of sex and life adjustment." And, as J. Moss and others have made clear, even when some sort of adjustment is achieved, the unmarried adult will remain isolated from society. It should not be surprising, therefore, that fully 28% of a sample of female college students expressed the opinion that they would be failures as women if they never married.[2]

What *is* surprising, in view of the many ways our society makes the unwed feel maladjusted, unhappy, and isolated, is that 88% of a sample of unmarried persons surveyed in a Roper poll, as cited by Brown, were either unconcerned or quite happy about their single state. (It is likely that since most of the sample—more than two-thirds—expected to marry eventually, they were not worried about the consequences of permanent deviation from social expectations.)

What happens to people after they get married? The amount and intensity of marital discontent far exceed what one might expect from an institution that professedly makes such a contribution to human happiness. The divorce rate for the United States—one divorce for every 3.6 marriages—certainly fails to inspire confidence. Moreover, the divorce rate does not provide a realistic estimate of marital unhappiness. Catholics, for example, can obtain divorces only under the most unusual circumstances; but it would be absurd to conclude that all Catholic marriages are happy. There are also the countless marriages preserved—or pickled—"for the sake of the children," or because divorce is too expensive, or to avoid adverse social consequences. Even in our enlightened age, the stigma that continues to be attached to divorce probably serves as a frequent deterrent. A news item from the *New York Times* provides an instructive illustration of this:

Court Sets Divorce "Etiquette"

> Toronto, April 3, 1962. Chief Justice J. C. McRuer of the Supreme Court of Ontario will not permit defendants in divorce actions to be addressed as ladies or gentlemen in his court. He gave notice yesterday that witnesses should simply refer to them as women or men.

In the words of one commentator, Barnes, "We have artificially constructed a society in which to be married is 'a good thing' and divorce is 'a bad thing,' although there is not a shred of scientific evidence to support either of these contentions." It should not be surprising, as Merton & Barber point out, that these social pressures eventually become internalized: "Since marriage is normatively defined as a presumptively continuing relation, it will be less readily terminated under the same load of dissatisfaction than the acquaintanceship. . . . The conception developed here. . .serves to correct the widely held but sociologically naive notion that the persistence of a particular social relation depends largely or wholly on the extent of personal satisfaction with it."

Divorce is not only disreputable, it is also viewed as symptomatic of mental illness—especially if repeated. To have more than three jobs in one's lifetime is not usually viewed as pathological, but "the fact that the mother [in a case being discussed by Guttmacher & Weihofen] had embarked on her fourth marriage is suggestive evidence of her own neurotic make-up."

The divorce rate as an index of marital unhappiness is unreliable, also, because of the many obstacles to divorce erected by our legal system. It is pitifully easy for two people in our society to get a marriage, but pitifully difficult for them to get a divorce. If this condition were reversed, so that marriage became more difficult to initiate and easier to terminate, the statistics would become more meaningful (and the institution itself less onerous). As long ago as 1901, J. A. Godfrey pointed out that, "The enforced continuance of an unsuccessful union is perhaps the most immoral thing which a civilized society ever countenanced." Holy wedlock becomes holy deadlock.

In many cases, the unhappy spouse is virtually forced to commit or feign adultery (often in collusion with his mate), because the state refuses to acknowledge less dramatic justifications for divorce. Perhaps this is what Havelock Ellis had in mind when he commented that "from the place they are entering beneath a garland of flowers, there is, on this side of death, no exit except through the trapdoor of a sewer."[3]

And what of the annulments, desertions, and separations that are divorces in everything but name? And what of the marriages that survive despite the unhappiness of one or both of the partners? We all know of marriages in which, in Reed's words, "the parties, after having been persuaded to endure an unhappy union for ten years or more, become so inured to the hardships and so hopeless of finding a more suitable relation, that they simply abandon the struggle and resign themselves to their unhappy state," and of marriages, as Goode said in 1961, in which "the couple has decided that staying together overrides other values, including each other's happiness and the psychological health of their children." If an accurate tally could be made, it would not be at all surprising to find that fewer than half of all marriages in our society are happy. There are two well-known surveys that support this conjecture: Hamilton found that fewer than 45% of the women interviewed were happily married; and Bossard & Boll indicated that the proportion of unsatisfying marriages was between one-third and one-fourth.[4] We also have evidence that marital happiness tends to decrease as the duration of the marriage increases.[5] One writer, Haire, has remarked that "any moderately intelligent person who goes about the world with his eyes open—who is willing to face the truths of life even if they are disagreeable—must be struck by the appalling frequency of unhappiness in marriage....Only one marriage in four may be judged as even tolerably successful." And an inspection of Swedish newspaper opinion led Westermarck, in 1936, to report a consensus that more than half of all Swedish marriages were unhappy. (It should be noted that we need not conclude from all this that there is something wrong with marriage as an institution. Groves, for example, argues that marital dissatisfaction, as manifested by the divorce rate, is rising because "matrimonial experience is moving toward higher standards and thereby making greater demands on the individual men and women." He presents no evidence in support of this interpretation.)

Some marriages probably should not so much be

called unhappy, as unfulfilling. One of the founders of the human actualization movement, Herbert Otto, puts it this way: "All too often, marriage results in a dull, stultifying routine, deadly to the growth processes of both partners....The three ingredients of such a marriage, which are the children, habit, and fear of social stigma, form an unhealthy glue, when it is the *only* glue which keeps a marriage together. There are more such marriages than we would care to admit. This is the tremendous clinical substratum of 'indifferent' or 'tolerable' marriages. This type of marriage unfortunately never reaches the counselor, but contributes to massive unhappiness, discontent, and finally the utter capitulation of a life endured, but not lived joyously."

Perhaps the most extreme kind of stultifying marriages can be characterized by the psychiatric phrase, "folie à deux"—a double pathology in which each partner satisfies the sick needs of the other, so that each passing day makes an eventual cure less likely. A sadist and a masochist might conceivably sustain a marital relationship over a considerable period of time, but few psychiatrists or psychologists would describe such a marriage as "happy."

In Otto's comments quoted above, reference was made to the strong force of habit. The role of this factor in keeping marriages intact has been overlooked by most commentators, but its significance appears to be undeniable. It is hard to break old habits, no matter how unrewarding they may have become. The thought of looking for a new partner may cause considerable apprehension, either because of emotional sloth (unwillingness to make the effort to establish a new relationship), or because of disdain for the fraud and foolishness that constitute such a large part of the dating game. If a second partner is already waiting in the wings, the existing marriage can be terminated with much less reluctance. In such a situation, the new partner should not be viewed as causing the marital bonds to be so oppressively tight, but rather as providing a sort of lubricant so that the bonds may be escaped with less discomfort.

We have not yet examined why marriage so frequently fails to promote human happiness. Why does marital bliss so often turn into marital blisters? Surely, one important element must be the constricting nature of the relationship. A number of studies suggest that marriage can stunt the development of one or both spouses, preventing the realization of their full potentialities as human beings. For example, there is the finding that individuals who are happily married are relatively more likely to be emotionally dependent.[6] Some readers may object that there is nothing wrong with dependency. Is it not preferable to aloofness, or impassivity? Perhaps so, but the juxtaposition of alternatives is inappropriate. We must note the important distinction between the ability or even the desire to become involved in interpersonal relationships, and the *need* for such relationships.[7] If an individual has so few resources that happiness is impossible without someone to lean on, then he is indeed in a state of grave emotional impoverishment. And the longer he uses this type of psychological crutch, the more likely he is to remain emotionally crippled. Thamm has recently made a similar point in an as yet unpublished sociological analysis of human relationships, which concludes that monogamistic pairings may create insecurity by virtually depriving the individual of sources of gratification other than the spouse; the greater the dependency, the greater the fear of loss. The marital happiness of those persons who are especially dependent is, therefore, especially likely to be short-lived. Also, the almost complete mutual absorption that characterizes so many marriages of the conventional romantic type may backfire. Morton Hunt, after listing some possible advantages of marriage, goes on to say, "The total merger of the selves over the years also may produce the irony of a relationship in which there is no longer anything to give each other, no unexpected riches to offer."

So much individuality must be sacrificed when one assumes the yoke of conventional matrimony[8] that we should not be surprised to learn from Reed that "the more highly developed the personality, the greater the difficulty of adjustment to marriage," nor, from Bernard, that "adjustment to the demands of marriage may greatly impair mental health," nor, from Locke, that the more conventional a person is, the more likely he or she is to be satisfied with marriage. In the words of a former judge of New York Children's Court, "Marriage does not as a matter of course emancipate; under some conditions it does the opposite—it enslaves."[9]

If the finding that married couples become more alike in behavior during their lives together[10] is confirmed, we should be alert to the obvious dangers of excessive intra-familial conformity and subsequent stagnation. There is also reason to believe that the mutual influence of spouses may serve to perpetuate attitudes more appropriate for past generations: we tend to marry, as Strauss points out, people whose opinions and personality characteristics resemble those of our parents. This "choice" serves, of course, to intensify the identification with one's spouse, so that the individuality of the married man or woman is blocked in two ways: by a submerging of the self in the personality of the spouse, and by the unthinking conservation of older ways of thinking.

With great wisdom, Samuel Hopkins Adams proposed the following contract to be obligatory for all newlyweds: "In and after the second year of the joint life of the contracting parties, they shall, circumstances permitting, separate for a period of not less than —— weeks nor more than —— months, during which time each shall honestly endeavor to reconstitute his or her own individuality." Adams did not specify the length of this respite; perhaps its duration should be 50 weeks per year, allowing the remaining two weeks for conjugal living—probably not long enough to do serious damage. Some such proposal might go far toward improving those "mutual suicide pacts" (Cadwallader, 1967) that we call marriages.

The economic costs of marriage—particularly after the birth of children (see p. 129)—are too obvious to require extended comment here. What may be less obvious is the likelihood, pointed out long ago by de LaPouge, that as societies grow richer, these costs will increase at a rate that may be greater than the rate of increase in per capita income.

Albert Ellis, in 1970, offered a partial summary of the evils of marriage that have been discussed thus far. Monogamy, he concluded, "leads to monotony, to restrictiveness, to possessiveness, to sexual starvation for many unmarried individuals, to the demise of romantic love, and to many other evils." (The present author would maintain that one of these suggested effects, the demise of romantic love, may be salutary.)

Despite—or maybe because of—the fact that marriage is more important for most wives than for most husbands, the evils of marriage may be felt more acutely by the wives; the husband is relatively more able to maintain and broaden his horizons through his work and the people with whom he comes in contact on the job. Our society has not yet outgrown its insistence that the best job for a woman is housewife. (As will be pointed out shortly, this limitation is especially difficult to escape when the wife becomes a mother.) The women's liberation movement has made significant progress in its attempt to equalize opportunities, but the situation continues to be flagrantly unjust. "It has been said that marriage diminishes man, which is often true; but almost always it annihilates woman."[11] Part of the problem is that the subservient status of the married woman is deeply embedded in our history. In 1840, Alexis de Tocqueville had this to say about American society:

> In America the independence of woman is irrecoverably lost in the bonds of matrimony....The Americans...require much abnegation on the part of women, and a constant sacrifice of her pleasures to her duties which is seldom demanded of her in Europe....When the time for choosing a husband is arrived, that cold and stern reasoning power which has been educated and invigorated by the free observation of the world, teaches an American woman that a spirit of levity and independence in the bonds of marriage is a constant subject of annoyance, not of pleasure; it tells her that the amusements of the girl cannot become the recreations of the wife, and that the sources of a married woman's happiness are in the home of her husband. As she clearly discerns beforehand the only road which can lead to domestic happiness, she enters upon it at once, and follows it to the end without seeking to turn back....[American women] attach

a sort of pride to the voluntary surrender of
their own will, and make it their boast to bend
themselves to the yoke, not to shake it off.

The vicious circle of which this voluntary servitude is
an integral part remains with us today. So long as society
continues its preferential emphasis on marriage and the
family, women will continue to be viewed as second-class
citizens in the "outside" world. The feelings of
inadequacy that are engendered may well force many
women, as Margaret Mead said in 1962, to "retreat into
fecundity," and to defend with ardor the wife-mother
role that may be the only one in which they can feel
comfortable and important. The kind of mentality
involved has often been called the *Kinder, Küche,
Kirche* (children, kitchen, church) mentality. It should be
obvious that the increasing control that women are
exercising over their own procreativity, while extremely
desirable, does not mean that marriage will cease to
represent a form of systematic exploitation. The "Three
K's" may be evolving into the "Three F's," the
contemporary wife being viewed, and perhaps even
viewing herself, as an instrument for feeding, flattering,
and having sexual intercourse with her husband (see the
comments of Cantarow and associates). The institution
of marriage, like institutions for criminals and the
mentally ill, may thus render some of its occupants
permanently unfit to function in freer settings. Betty
Friedan and Kate Millett have both made interesting
reflections on this point. The disadvantages of marriage
are likely to be exacerbated if the couple has children.
Flügel points out, "To some extent, the individual
inevitably sacrifices himself in becoming a parent," thus
approaching the sorry plight of the salmon, whose
spawning is a form of suicide. It is the woman, of course,

who suffers most cruelly from society's emphasis on parenthood. "Having a child," Simone de Beauvoir writes, "is enough to paralyze a woman's activity completely." Another commentator, Spiro, spelled out the nature of this paralysis in 1955: "Since the woman must bear, and hence rear, children, she has little time or opportunity for other than domestic activities. Once freed from the responsibility of rearing children and the manifold domestic chores (cleaning, cooking, laundering, and so on) attendant upon such care, she could devote her energies to...more creative areas of life." Or, in the somewhat irreverent but highly relevant words of Betty Rollin, "If God were still speaking to us in a voice we could hear ... He would probably say, 'Be fruitful. Don't multiply.' "

But, it may be argued, creativity is less important than happiness. While this might seem to be a valid objection, Terman's classic study of marital happiness has shown that "if there are individual marriages that are made more happy by the presence of children, these appear to be offset by other marriages that are made less happy." Feldman's more recent study goes further, providing evidence that married couples are less happy after they have children than before, and are less happy than couples that have never had children;[12] both spouses, moreover, reported negative personality changes after becoming parents. (There were, of course, exceptions to these generalizations.) By way of provisional summary, it may be asserted that freeing women from child-rearing and other household tasks would increase their value to society without reducing their happiness.

Reference has already been made to the fact that children, once of value economically, are now more realistically viewed as financial liabilities. Rollin points out that "With the average cost of a middle-class child figured conservatively at $30,000 (not including college), any parent knows that the only people who benefit economically from children are manufacturers of consumer goods."

The frustrations and restrictions of being a parent may often remain unacknowledged, either becuase of a lack of insight or for fear of being regarded as a misfit—a monster so cold-blooded as to resent the burdens of child-rearing. "Man's primary function," ·according to one early pronouncement, "is to create food and wealth for the community, while woman's primary function is to bear and rear the children of the community."[13] Still, there are circumstances, such as the interviewer's promise of anonymity, under which the mother will admit that child-rearing is an unwelcome task, to be finished as soon as possible. In one survey, most of the parents (usually the mothers) expressed the desire that their children grow up quickly so that parental careers might be begun or resumed.[14] And in one of the most searching inquiries into this problem that has yet been published, Alice Rossi observes that "for many women the personal outcome of experience in the parent role is not a higher level of maturation but the negative outcome of a depressed sense of self-worth, if not actual personality deterioration. There is considerable evidence that this is more prevalent than we recognize." Rossi cites reports of both lower-class and middle-class women. Likewise, another study, conducted by Gass, has revealed that the majority of a sample of upper-middle-class women had obtained little satisfaction from child-rearing and were delighted to be freed from this confining task.

This is not to say, of course, that reproductive responsibilities are invariably onerous. But it remains true that about 10% of all females admitted to psychiatric hospitals are suffering from "profound emotional disturbances associated with child bearing,"[15] that, according to Wainwright, fatherhood may precipitate mental illness, and that the birth of a first child creates a serious crisis in the lives of many—if not most—apparently normal married couples.[16] It seems, then, that the patter of little feet is not an unmixed blessing.

Fortunately, increasing numbers of persons of both sexes have been liberating themselves from the stultifying sex-role patterns of times past, and it may not be much longer before the stereotyped household drudge becomes a straw woman. But a particularly dangerous trap still appears to be all but unavoidable. On the one hand, as Marya Mannes pointed out in 1964, "if the creative woman has children, she must pay for this indulgence with a long burden of guilt, for her life will be split three ways between them and her husband and her work." On the other hand, Parsons (in Parsons & Bales) has suggested that those parents who have no role other than the parent-role may unduly prolong the dependency of their children.

Despite occasional claims to the contrary, there is nothing particularly noble about the sacrifices parents make for their children—sacrifices that are all the more pathetic if they are unacknowledged or unfelt. Does it make much sense for one generation to sacrifice itself for the next, when that next generation will, in turn, sacrifice itself for its successor? It is hard to imagine anything more futile. And how vicious it is for parents to attempt to emotionally blackmail their children with continual references to fingers that have been worked to the bone. The children did not ask to be born, and the prodigious supportive efforts of which their parents boast are usually little more than what the law requires.

These misgivings are compounded when inquiry is made into the effectiveness of parental attempts at child-rearing. As suggested earlier, children can thrive in properly operated institutions. But this is only part of the story. Family-reared children probably do *less* well than they would if they were brought up in truly adequate institutions. In other words, the assertion is now being made here (albeit tentatively) that parents generally do more harm than good. This notion is by no means a new one. Catherine the Great, according to Calverton, had "endeavored to carry out the old theory of taking away children from their parents and educating them in government schools and colleges. She was eager to have children escape the oppression of the family, the parental stupidities and affections." In fact, the theory can be traced back at least as far as Plato's *Republic*.

What is the justification for this claim that most parents are doing an inadequate job? As might be expected, there are several justifications. These may be conveniently divided into two categories, although the reader will note a certain degree of overlap. Category I has to do with the consequences of being brought up by persons unfit to serve as parents. Category II includes those problems inherent in the standard parent-child relationship.

I. When parents are unfit. In view of the impossibility of conducting formal experiments designed to measure the effects of bad parenting, we are forced to rely on case studies, on clinical impressions, and on generalizations from informally gathered data. Among many other considerations, we must particularly bear in mind that the child of pathological or inept parents is typically forced to bear the burden of a poor genetic endowment as well as a poor environment. Nevertheless, the observations that follow, impressionistic and subjective though some of them may be, may at least serve to remind the reader that not all people share our society's current glorification of the family.

According to Strecker, a leading psychiatrist, "in the vast majority of case histories of the men who were rejected or discharged from the armed forces because of 'neuro-psychiatric tendencies,' a 'mom' is at fault." He reports, too, that "momism in childhood was the basic, underlying cause" of 80% of the cases of alcoholism he encountered.[17] Of course, not all mothers are the neurotic, overprotective monsters designated by Strecker (and, earlier, by Philip Wylie) as "moms." Still, the author of a textbook on the family suggests that society's needs might better be served if, instead of a marriage license, a mother's license were required before a woman would be permitted to have children.[18]

Some writers go much further. Haire: "One sometimes wonders whether the average parents are not the least fit persons in the world to bring up their own child." Schmalhausen, in 1930: "Family life. . .is about the very best raw material which the psychopathologist has at his disposal for studying intimately every kind of idiocy and imbecility, every phase of insanity . . . . Family life doth make idiots and lunatics of us all. . . .It creates, perpetuates, glorifies emotional bondage." De Pomerai: "Scarcely one parent in a thousand is really capable of efficiently rearing and training a child. . . .The average child is happier and far better off in a nursery school or properly organized educational institution than it is in its own home. . . .If private homes have been responsible for a gigantic crop of physical defects, they have been responsible for an even greater harvest of warped personalities, suppressed abilities, and unnecessary antagon-isms." It is not difficult to share the sense of futility and entrapment Schmalhausen must have felt when he wrote, "Are parents to be pitied? Yes, I think so. Pitied and shot." His conclusion is echoed by the more recent recommendation that what some children need is a "par-entectomy."[19]

The "gigantic crop of physical defects" mentioned above is one claim that has been amply documented. The *Journal of the American Medical Association* reported in 1962 that beatings by parents may cause more deaths among children than leukemia, cystic fibrosis, or mus-cular dystrophy, and perhaps as many as are caused by automobile accidents. Current statistics indicate a total of approximately 50,000 cases of child abuse in the United States per year.[20]

This summary of the consequences of irresponsible parenthood is by no means exhaustive,[21] and yet, as of 1942, one of the standard textbooks on the family, by Becker & Hill, held that "a poor home is better than none at all." It is significant that this statement does not appear in the 1948 edition of the book, where it is replaced by the less extreme assertion that "it is better for a child to have an intact home, even though not a very good one, than to feel himself differentiated from other children as a child without a home." (This latter position, which properly attributes to social factors a ma-jor part of the maladjustments of institutionalized chil-dren, will be reconsidered in the next chapter.)

We do not, and cannot, know the number of men and women in the United States whose psychological problems render them unfit for parenthood. But we may assume (see p. 144) that at least half of our adult population suffers from some form or other of emo-tional disturbance; and we may further assume that children ought not to be dependent for their upbringing on these disturbed individuals, if a viable alternative were available. But before examining the possible alternatives, we must direct our attention to those families—infrequent though they may be—in which the parents both appear capable of doing an acceptable job of child-rearing.

II. Problems inherent in the nuclear family structure. The nuclear family, consisting of a husband, wife, and dependent children, may be, by its very nature, an inadequate locus of child-rearing. Even the best of parents is unlikely to be good enough to counteract the obstacles to growth and maturity that are embedded in this system.

The conclusions Margaret Mead drew in 1939, based on years of cross-cultural studies of family structures, are especially worthy of consideration. "The reward of our type of family is specialization of affection...but at the price of many individuals' preserving through life the attitudes of dependent children, of ties between parents and children which successfully defeat the children's attempts to make other adjustments, of necessary choices made unnecessarily poignant because they become issues in an intense emotional relationship. Perhaps these are too heavy prices to pay for a specialization of emotion which might be brought about in other ways ..." And, she continues, "...it would be desirable to mitigate, at least in some slight measure, the strong role which parents play in children's lives, and so eliminate one of the most powerful accidental factors in the choices of any individual life....In our ideal picture of the freedom of the individual and the dignity of human relations it is not pleasant to realize that we have developed a form of family organization which often cripples the emotional life, and warps and confuses the growth of many individuals' power to consciously live their own lives." Furthermore, there is considerable clinical evidence to support her point that the close relationship between parent and child in our society is such that "submission to the parent or defiance of the parent may become the dominating pattern of a life-time."

Mead is, of course, not the only student of society who has found fault with our family arrangements. Broom & Selznick comment that "in Western society, where the natural parents are usually the primary source of attention and care, the child's anxiety is probably greater than in societies where more people care for him." (This anxiety may be related to the fear-love complex discussed in a previous chapter.) And Calverton & Schmalhausen assert that mothers often warp the lives of their children with their affection, hindering rather than helping them in the struggle for individual fulfillment.

Although psychologists have generally confined their interest in family pathology to cases in which gross mental disorder is present, a few have taken a broader view. For example, no less an authority than Jean Piaget has observed that the standard method of parental child-rearing emphasizes submission, rather than cooperation, and thus retards the development of objectivity and rationality.[22]

It is reasonable to expect that girls will be particularly affected by the home, because they typically maintain closer ties with their parents. This differential effect might help to explain the finding of Crandall and associates that girls (but not boys) who receive the most parental affection have lower levels of academic achievement than do those less favored by their parents. This finding is in accord with Piaget's position, although it should be obvious that definitive proof is still lacking.

Conclusive evidence is likewise lacking with respect to the Oedipus complex. This is not the place for a detailed account of the intense anxiety and conflict presumably generated by the child's erotic interest in the opposite-sexed parent and the hostility he simultaneously feels toward the same-sexed parent, but two elements of Freud's theory are quite relevant in the present context. First, Freud asserted that the Oedipus complex is inescapable within the framework of the nuclear family. Second, he stated that all neuroses have their roots in the Oedipus complex. If both of these difficult-to-prove statements are correct, then it follows that a neurosis-free society cannot exist if children are customarily brought up by their parents. While it may be too extreme to say that neurosis will disappear when current child-rearing patterns have been modified, it may still be reasonable to expect a dramatic reduction in the incidence of this debilitating disorder.[23] At the very least, we can probably accept anthropologist William Stephens' suggestion in 1961 that in societies in which there are other mother-figures to absorb the child's sexual interest, there would be less sexual interest in the biological mother. It also makes sense that "the mother is often the last person suited to deal with the child's deepest moral problems, because she is already the cause and center of his deepest guilt feelings."[24] And finally, we have a cross-cultural study conducted by Whiting, Kluckhohn & Anthony suggesting that the more intensely an infant is loved by its mother, the more emotionally dependent it will be upon her, and the more hostile and envious it will be toward persons perceived as rivals. A finding that appears to be congruent with the foregoing is that family-reared children, when compared to institutionalized children, were more anxious, shy, easily discouraged, and dependent upon praise.[25] Perhaps it is time to become less concerned about the dangers of "hospital-ism" (the term used by some writers to denote the effects of institutionalization), and more concerned about the menace of "familism."

Another body of evidence demonstrating the negative effects that family-rearing may have on children has to do with the consequences of divorce. It is undeniably true that divorce can be an extremely unfortunate expe-rience for the children involved. For this reason, the man and woman in an unstable marriage are well ad-vised to delay starting a family until their difficulties have been resolved. But this recommendation in no way implies that divorce should be avoided "for the sake of the children." According to William Goode, in 1962, "The best opinion and data insist that children of dis-cord or separation suffer greater disadvantages than those whose parents actually divorce." Another writer, Hutchinson, suggests that in some cases, for the sake of the children, divorce should be compulsory. To give but one example from the research literature, a survey of college students revealed that those who were the offspring of unhappily but still married parents rated lower in adjustment to the opposite sex than did those whose parents had divorced.[26]

For all of the reasons mentioned in the preceding pages, we may conclude this portion of the discussion with the following words: "It is not strange that the child guidance specialists, confronted with case after case of children victimized by parental influence, grow skeptical as to the value of the home as a modern means of child training." These are not the words of a contemporary young radical. They were written, more than 30 years ago, in 1941, by Groves, one of the most respected scholars in the field of marriage and the family.

This discussion of the negative consequences of the

family-rearing of children has focused, quite naturally, on the children themselves. But a few words need to be added concerning some possible broader consequences of conventional upbringing. The undesirability and virtual inevitability of familial transmission of attitudes from one generation to the next have already been mentioned (p. 124). Critics of the uniformity alleged to result from institutional life might better consider the implosion of me-too-ism so often noted in current American society. Why are so many family-reared citizens replicas of one another, carbon copies of their parents, or docile sheep in the contemporary version of follow-the-leader? Are these arch-conformists being created *in spite of* our traditional family system, or *because* of it?

(We should also remember that familial pressures toward conformity are not unilateral. Moore has pointed out how children, influenced by the mass media, may proceed to exercise influence over their parents.)

Our method of bringing up children may not only inhibit individual growth, but inhibit social progress as well. As Robert Morison has suggested, the fact that the average child spends his first five or six years "in the bosom of his family...is primarily responsible for the relative fixity of the socio-economic class structure of a country like the United States....The family is relatively poor at assimilating and transmitting new knowledge essential to survival in a rapidly moving world."[27] Of course, a major determinant of our class structure is the inequitable distribution of income. As the rich get richer and the poor get poorer, their offspring are progressively less likely to come into meaningful contact with one another. Democratic myths to the contrary, we are thus approaching a sort of modern-day caste system, with all of the human degradation and wasted potential that such a system entails. To some observers, such as Ryder, it is becoming increasingly obvious that "strong family relationships. . .are incompatible with the rational allocation of human resources."

Political inequities may also be fostered by our present family system. In Reich's words, "The authoritarian state has a representative in every family, the father; in this way he becomes the state's most valuable tool."[28] Although Goode does not endorse this position, in his 1966 paper he cites the finding that children are more likely to exhibit more democratic social behavior if they spend a larger proportion of their time with their peers than with their parents. And he alludes to "a speculation often made by social philosophers and sociologists," that individuals who are reared largely in family settings, whence they derive most of their satisfactions, tend to overvalue the ingroup and "treat outsiders as of little value."

But perhaps the most disconcerting effect of all is expressed in Margaret Mead's comment that the intense mother-child relationship that characterizes our nuclear family structure "may be the most efficient way to produce a character suited to lifelong monogamous marriage."[29] Still another vicious circle is thus in operation, each marriage—no matter how unsatisfactory—helping to perpetuate the marital institution itself.

It should be apparent that America's allegiance to marriage-and-children-for-all can become disastrous to society at large. Many of the reasons to fear the cultural consequences of monogamania, or familiphilia, have been spelled out in the preceding pages, but two more may be mentioned here. First, in Barnes's words, "the pressures on our young people toward marriage are greater than any pressure they may feel to contribute significantly to the progress of our society." Second, it is doubtful that the population crisis confronting the world today can be adequately dealt with until this highly influential country abandons its present pro-marriage orientation.[30] (We shall return to this point in the next chapter.)

Even granting that marriage has outlived its sexual, economic, and child-rearing utility, one might still maintain that the marital relationship exerts a stabilizing or maturing influence on husband and wife. Without marriage, perhaps desertions would occur after the slightest adversity or disagreement. There would be none of the feelings of permanence, or personal responsibility, that separate man from the lower animals. And there would be little opportunity for the development of love and unselfish devotion. Let us examine some of these allegations.

It is a vast oversimplification to state that adversity strengthens the will or matures the personality. Indeed, the psychological and psychiatric literature abounds in reports of adversity producing exactly the opposite effects. And even if adversity *were* useful, surely enough is encountered in our daily life so that marriage need not be inflicted upon us for this purpose. We do not force people—even for their own good—to stay on a job after they wish to change, and yet we restrict the far more important freedom to terminate interpersonal relationships. The gradual liberalization of our divorce laws is an indication that society is finally coming to recognize the immorality of enforced lifelong relationships.

Is adherence to one partner a sign, or a cause, of mental health? Not necessarily. As Kubie pointed out, in 1948, "Every analyst knows that monogamous fidelity can sometimes be the result of free, healthy, conscious choice, and at other times an escape from profound neurotic guilt and fear." Havelock Ellis anticipated this observation many years ago, commenting that a corset exerts the same kind of influence on physical responsibility as does formal marriage on moral responsibility. Also worth remembering is the fact, noted by Livingstone as far back as 1899, that non-marital relationships can be remarkably stable: "the necessity for mutual kindness and forbearance [instead of legal restraints] establishes a condition that is the best guarantee of permanency." Some people, at least, will try harder to make a relationship worth continuing if they know it is not going to continue automatically. One may also rebut the mental-health claim by pointing out that the mutual dependency that so often accompanies marriage is certainly not conducive to mental health.

Another pro-marriage argument, occasionally encountered, is based on demographic statistics that married people live longer than the unmarried. But this finding can be readily explained without recourse to the proposition that marriage causes longevity. For example, the statistics do not take into account the likelihood that ill individuals may decide not to marry or may not be able to find partners. As long as such selective factors are ignored, the demographic data will remain difficult to interpret. (Furthermore, Berkson points out that the statistics themselves may be grossly inaccurate because of systematic errors in data collection.) The "better wed than dead" viewpoint (as expressed by *Changing Times* in 1971), is also challenged by Jourard, who goes so far as to assert that marriage has fostered disease by creating stresses which lower the individual's resistance to germs and other noxious agents.

We must also be careful to avoid misinterpreting the information, noted by Nelson, that single persons have a higher suicide rate than do married persons. Can this be viewed as evidence for the superiority of marriage? If so, logic would compel us to discourage people from going to college, because of the relatively higher suicide rate among college students (also indicated by Nelson). As a matter of fact, the higher suicide rate among the unmarried can be easily attributed to the feelings of alienation that a marriage-pushing society instills among those who deviate from the norm.[31]

Some Final Comments

The ultimate test of the hypothesis that marriage is no longer a necessary or desirable institution would involve a large-scale experiment in which societies having identical characteristics except for the presence or absence of marriage would be compared in terms of cultural progress, average level of mental health, or whatever other variables are deemed important. Obviously, such an experiment can never be conducted. In lieu of this ideal form of assessment, we are left with three options.

(1) We can compare societies differing in marriage rate, and draw tentative conclusions as to whether or not a very high marriage rate is "better" than a lower one. Systematic work along these lines has not yet been done, but Barnes pointedly informs us that only 2% of the adult population of India is unmarried, compared to 19% in the Scandinavian countries. The corresponding rate for the United States is 8%.

(2) We can study the social experiments in marital reform that *have* taken place, even though these have generally been on a rather small scale (see Chapter VI).

(3) Finally, we can consider the speculations that have been offered by individuals who have concerned

themselves with these matters. One particularly specious defense of marriage as an institution involves the contention that the institution has been supported by everybody except a few fools and crackpots. But a considerable number of writers and thinkers (could they *all* have been fools or crackpots?) have very seriously questioned the value of marriage. The following collection of quotations is not intended to be persuasive. The ideas expressed have not been proven and do not readily lend themselves to rigorous testing. They are presented here simply in an attempt to counterbalance the equally unproven pro-marriage messages that reach us from all sides.

"Individuals," says de Beauvoir, "are not to be blamed for the failure of marriage; it is...the institution itself, perverted as it has been from the start."[32] Shaw, in his preface to *Getting Married*—a play as timely now as when it was written sixty years ago—writes that "home life as we understand it is no more natural to us than a cage is to a cockatoo. Its grave danger to the nation lies in its narrow views, its petty tyrannies, its false social pretenses, its endless grudges and squabbles." Calverton (in Calverton & Schmalhausen) asserts that monogamy has been "inhumanitarian in every aspect of its evolution....Its influence upon life has been cruel and vicious." When asked about the most suitable age at which a man should marry, Francis Bacon replied, "The young man not yet, the old man not at all."[33] Schmalhausen in 1928 observed that "marriage used to mean living together until death do us part. It now means living apart until death do bring us together. Marriage is a fascinating study in compensatory behavior offsetting an unbearable sense of personal inadequacy. Marriage is the most complicated of the psychoneuroses." And according to sociologist M. L. Cadwallader, in a 1967 paper,

> Contemporary marriage is a wretched institution. More often than not it turns out to be a personal calamity for the happy couple....It spells the end of voluntary affection, of love freely given and joyously received. The relationship becomes constricting, corrosive, and contractual....The institution of marriage... has failed.

The disintegration that Pitirim Sorokin, and others, predicted for marriage need not be viewed with alarm. If it does take place, it could have deep and far-reaching positive consequences for all of society. To a very great extent, we are what society makes us. At least half of the American population is, to some degree, emotionally disturbed.[34] According to Goldhamer & Marshall, at least one out of every ten of us will be hospitalized at one time or another because of serious psychological difficulties. And all this in a society with marriage, maternal love, and filial devotion. Let those who proclaim what awful things will accompany the development of nonmarital forms of human relationship ponder the awful things that have accompanied marriage itself. The burden of proof concerning the value of marriage in contemporary society rests on those who choose to take a pro-marriage position.

Marriage—or at least our current version of it—reduces many adults' chances for finding happiness and attaining maturity. It entails a type of child-rearing that reduces the chances of many children for happiness and maturity, creating in them feelings of dependency, inadequacy, and insecurity that impel them to marry and to infect *their* children with the same self-destructive feelings. Its direct and indirect costs to society are enormous and insidious. For these reasons, marriage can be viewed as a social disease. Fortunately, it is not too late for the disease to be cured.

VI

Permissive Matrimony: Proposals for the Future

To CRITICIZE A SOCIAL institution without meaningful positive recommendations for change is little more than a futile exercise. The proposals that follow are intended to eliminate the existing system of coercive matrimony, without creating new forms of coercion or a chaotic absence of norms.

It may be argued that the remedy lies not in encouraging the replacement of conventional marital relationships, but rather in strengthening existing arrangements. Such a conclusion, I believe, would be disastrous. Marriage, for most people, has outlived its usefulness and is doing more harm than good. The solution is not to make divorces more difficult to obtain, but to recognize the so-called divorce problem for what it is: a symptom of the marriage problem. And to get rid of a symptom, you try to do something about the underlying illness. By way of analogy, if a child fails to thrive despite daily beatings from his parents, is the solution to increase the severity of the beatings? No, if a particular practice does not seem to be working, it is appropriate to ask if the practice is necessary. Similarly, it is appropriate now to ask: Is marriage necessary?

147

I propose a system of "permissive matrimony" within which individuals can choose, within very broad limits, the types of human relationships they wish to experience. All individuals (subject to a few restrictions to be noted later), would be permitted to choose freely from among the following options:

    I. Conventional Monogamy
   II. Modified monogamy
  III. Non-monogamous matrimony
  IV. Non-marital relationships

In the pages that follow, these alternatives will be examined, along with their probable consequences.

I. *Conventional Monogamy*

Little needs to be said at this point concerning the current mode of male-female and parent-child relationships. Anyone who wishes, for reasons of religious commitment, moral beliefs, or personality, to enter upon a conventional marriage would be perfectly free to do so—provided, of course, that he can find a willing partner. The fact that "permissive matrimony" does include this option should lay to rest any claims that I am advocating the abolition of conventional marriage. However, if the analysis in the foregoing chapters is correct, it is reasonable to assume that progressively fewer people would avail themselves of this particular option, because of the availability of more attractive alternatives, and that conventional marriage would evolve out of existence. The social and psychological consequences of this gradual disappearance need to be put into proper perspective, and will be shortly. For now, it can be said that the inconvenience of adjusting to new ways of life are likely to be quite minor in comparison with the insults on human dignity that seem to be intrinsic in the existing system.

II. *Modified Monogamy*[1]

There are many ways in which monogamy might be modified in order to reflect more faithfully the realities of the twentieth century. Most of these have been tried, but it is doubtful if any have been fairly tested.

Non-exclusive Monogamy. This refers to a marital arrangement by which one man and one woman are married to each other, but are under no obligation to refrain from sexual (or other) relationships with other persons. Adultery, no longer a legal ground for divorce, would, rather, be viewed as a normal and acceptable diversion. The frequency and degree of institutionalization of adulterous behavior might vary from infrequent, almost accidental encounters, to regularly scheduled evenings of "swinging." Little is known about this latter development. Palson & Palson do note that the movement appears to be growing, and that it generally has no adverse consequences on the marriages of the people involved. One sign of evolution is the virtual disappearance of the term "wife-swapping," with its connotation of male proprietorship. The essence of swinging is that both parties to the marriage may enjoy, and should have the right to enjoy, sexual activities with like-minded couples. (It should be noted, however, that the concept of nonexclusive matrimony does not necessarily entail a regular pattern of partner-swapping. The concept does entail considerable freedom for both partners, with an absence of punishment or disapproval from one another or from

society at large.) Incidentally, contemporary legal sta-
tutes against adultery appear to be anachronistic: "The
gist of the crime [of adultery] is the danger of introduc-
ing spurious heirs into a family."[2] As contraceptive
methods continue to improve, this danger will become
less and less real.

Child-free Monogamy.[3] This marital situation is similar
to the status quo, but minus the child-rearing function.
If it is true that children are being brought up, in many
cases, by the people least suited to do so (i.e., their parents), and if it is true that children reduce, in many
cases, the marital and/or individual satisfaction of their
parents, then it follows that marriage could be improved,
as an institution, if it were less closely tied to the child-
rearing function. Cutting the apron strings can be beneficial to the people on both ends of the string. The children of individuals selecting this option would be placed
in institutions shortly after birth, or would be adopted,
or would be brought up communally. (For a more detailed account of child-rearing, see below.)

Contractual Monogamy. As its name implies, contractual
monogamy involves the recognition of marriage as a civil
contract. As such, the relationship could be terminable
without recourse to complicated legal or religious procedures, or unseemly accusations. At least two types of
contractual arrangements can be envisaged. In the first
of these, the marriage is automatically terminable by mutual consent. Alternatively, a term contract can be agreed
upon, with the option of renewal at regular intervals.
This latter proposal is by no means novel. In ancient
Japan, as Havelock Ellis points out, five-year marriage
contracts were not uncommon. Its advocates have included Goethe, and a member of the court of Louis

XIV, who recommended it after observing that marriage was a "betrayal of the self, an unnatural compulsion" [cited by Lewinsohn]. The duration of the contract can either be set by law or can be specified by the individuals concerned. In 1966, Cadwallader proposed a period of one or two years. The contract can even be lifelong, differing from conventional marriage in that the terms of the contract are established by the partners, rather than by society.

The 1972 best-seller, *Open Marriage*, by the O'Neills, should be mentioned at this point, because it suggests a contract designed to give both partners a greater degree of autonomy and individuality than is usually available within traditional marriage. If the book's popularity is any indication, there are a great many people who feel trapped by what they perceive to be the rigidities of conventional marriage. Although the book's underlying thesis is quite conservative—with its insistence on the necessity for monogamy because of mankind's alleged need for "structure"—its proposals can be strongly recommended to those who want something less constricting than a "closed marriage," and yet do not feel prepared for any of the less conventional options.

Trial Marriage. Trial marriage means many things to many people, but its various forms appear to be subsumable within the general category of modified monogamy. One type of trial marriage involves the couple living together for as long as they wish, or for a stipulated period of time, after which they either separate or become married in the conventional sense. For example, Vance Packard, who has argued against term marriage because of the constant pressure he believes would be felt by both partners, has proposed the alternative of a two-year "confirmation" period before the taking of formal nuptial vows. An attractive variant is to permit childless couples to dissolve their relationships at any time by mutual consent, after a nine-month separation. This, in essence, is Judge Benjamin Lindsey's concept of "companionate marriage."[4] In a very real sense, all marriages are trial marriages—a fact that Judge Lindsey was among the first to appreciate. It should be noted that the Lindsey proposal represents a fusion of "contractual" and "trial" marriage.

The two preceding options share the property of solubility by mutual consent. Another type of arrangement would permit unilateral termination. This possibility is not so heartless as it may seem. As has been pointed out earlier, a marriage with only one willing partner is scarcely a marriage at all. What self-respecting person would want to continue a marriage in which the spouse remained solely because of legal, social, or psychological duress? Unilateral termination has proven its practicability in Arabic countries (where, however, as Stephens noted in 1963, the prerogative is exclusively male), and in the Soviet Union. The practice was abolished in the latter country, for reasons that may be instructive to persons interested in re-introducing it here: (1) "post-card" divorces created considerable confusion, because administrative inefficiency resulted in numerous instances of divorced people not knowing they had been divorced; (2) the construction of state-operated child-care institutions, necessary for the marital reforms envisaged by the Soviets, was unfortunately accorded a lower priority than the construction of steel mills and other industrial plants; (3) some highly placed officials believed that the new opinions and attitudes underlying the Revolution could best be transmitted to the next generation via the parents; and (4) the government eventually terminated its liberal policy on "moral" grounds—quite possibly based on a steadily decreasing birth rate that was incompatible with national expansionist goals.[5] Obviously, these considerations would be irrelevant in countries with efficient communication systems and with other goals and other priorities.

Quarternary Marriage. In the quarternary marriage version, two married couples and their offspring cohabit, with the goals of companionship, division of labor, and increasing the number of adult role-models available to the children. Mate-swapping may or may not occur. As Ravich has pointed out, this sort of arrangement is most likely to succeed if begun early, before the two couples have had a chance to develop incompatible life-styles.

The Three-generation Family. Most of the foregoing options (and some of those that follow) can be readily incorporated within a multi-generational framework. The "extended family" and its variants, so frequently described by cultural anthropologists, have numerous obvious advantages. With children living in the midst of grandparents as well as parents, the number of adult role-models is increased, parental ties may be beneficially weakened, a more realistic perception of the aged may be attained, and the elderly would find themselves in environments less morbid and more conducive to self-respect than the typical old-age home. But these advantages may be neutralized by the social stagnation likely to ensue. The roadblocks to progress that appear to be inevitable consequences of parental upbringing could be magnified by the added conservative pressures provided by grandparents. It is significant that none of the societies usually referred to as "advanced" displays this pattern of family life. So long as the three-generation family is merely one option among many, its positive features will remain attractive. But if the option were to become the norm, the results might well be disastrous.

III. *Non-monogamous Matrimony*

Perhaps the exclusivity that makes for boredom and stultification could be mitigated by recourse to multiple marital arrangements. Three alternatives present themselves, although they may not always be separable in practice.

Polygamy. Polygamy, of either the polygynous or polyandrous variety, would obviously increase the number of permissible mates. As has already been mentioned (see p. 19), fewer than 20% of the world's societies have established monogamy as the preferred form of marriage. Although this figure may be somewhat misleading, because the populations of the various societies are not taken into account, and because the actual practice of polygamy may be restricted to the wealthy minority who can afford it, we would still be rather arrogant to claim that our particular marital customs are more "natural" than any others. Nevertheless, no advocacy of polygamy will be presented here. Too often, the multiple husbands or wives can become mere possessions, rather than independent persons. Although it may be possible for polygamous partners to achieve a greater degree of individuality than is usually obtainable in monogamy (because marital relationships might be less all-encompassing), the functions which such unions would serve in contemporary Western society are even more tenuous than those allegedly served by monogamy.[6] Only under very unusual economic circumstances, or as a result of a large discrepancy in the male-female ratio, might such groupings be feasible in the United States.

Group Marriage and Communes. These objections may be less applicable, however, to what has been called "group marriage"—the simultaneous practice of polygamy and polygyny, in which every man in the group is married to every woman. Group marriage, representing an attenuation of traditional bonds, has attracted considerable attention in recent years. A number of experiments in group marriage are currently in progress, and it should soon be possible to evaluate the effects of these attempts to reduce exclusivity and possessiveness. Some insight is already available from reports describing early "Utopian" experiments that embodied some form of group marriage. One of the better-documented of these, which took place in Oneida, New York, during the last century, was characterized by the communal upbringing of children and a doctrine of "complex marriage" that closely resembled what we would call group marriage. What was life like in the Oneida Community? "Morbid sex interest, violent passion, extreme sentimentality, and jealousy were said to have been largely eliminated. Spontaneous, mutual, frank, and comradely social relations between men and women were made easier. . . . The rate of nervous disease in the community was considerably below the average outside. Such at least are the results reported by Havelock Ellis and certain others who have studied the community."[7]

The experiment continued for 40 years, terminating primarily, in the words of Hart & Hart, "because of growing social tension between the sexual behavior patterns of the community and of the outside world." (To this should be added the important point that the founder of the community, John Noyes, failed to make adequate provision for an effective successor.)

This would be an appropriate juncture at which to discuss the relatively new, highly publicized "commune" movement. However, no extended analysis will be attempted, for two reasons. First, the communes have had insufficient time to develop; a full generation must elapse before a valid evaluation of the consequences and the viability of communal living in the United States can be undertaken.[8] Second, the relationship between the commune movement and this book's inquiry into marital reform is by no means clear. Some communes do represent attempts to establish group marriage, others may be better understood as alliances among monogamous couples, and still others represent combinations of these. (A similar lack of homogeneity concerning child-rearing practices may be observed.) For our purposes, it is enough to state that communal arrangements, however these may be defined, should be viewed as perfectly acceptable, and stigma-free, options.

Apart from the rather blurred picture that emerges from communes, there are in existence a number of more specific attempts to establish group marriages.[9] What can be said about these? Group marriage does serve to increase the number of legally recognizable (if not yet recognized) sexual partners, and does seem to promote feelings of community and closeness (perhaps because the participants feel estranged from the outside society that views them as renegades; with increasing social acceptance, the interpersonal bonds within the group might well diminish in intensity). Also, there is evidence (see p. 4) that in multiple-mating arrangements, the fertility rate declines—obviously an advantage in an overcrowded world.[10] Still another potential advantage is suggested by Millett's comment that "given woman's extraordinary biological potentiality for sexual arousal and pleasure, no form of sexual association would have satisfied it less than monogamy or polygyny; none more than group marriage." But despite these important considerations, group marriage would probably still perpetuate many of the evils of the existing system: the social coercion to marry, and the legal and "familial" pressures to maintain marital bonds even after these have ceased to be satisfying. Those who object to marriage because of the enforced togetherness that is usually entailed would find no respite in group marriage.

Before proceeding to the next general category, we should note that the various non-monogamous forms share the advantage of offering to the offspring an enlarged circle of companionship and a corresponding reduction in dependency upon one's biological parents. The children would thus be less vulnerable to the trauma of sudden separation resulting from parental death, divorce, etc., and would also be less susceptible to the sibling rivalry that may result from insufficient or inequitable adult attention.[11]

IV. *Non-marital Relationships*

Included in this category are all those types of relationships which, by virtue of their freedom from legal, religious, or social constraints, are non-binding and readily terminable. The term "free love" has the same denotation but suffers from misleading connotations. In the first place, reference to "love" is inappropriate, because that emotion may play no role in the establishment or continuation of the relationship. "Free sex" would be a preferable term, except that "free" may imply, to some, an irresponsible exploitation that does not require the consent of both partners.

The precise nature of the non-marital relationships cannot be detailed, because their scope is as unlimited as the number of human relationships in which people may find themselves, and is as broad as human ingenuity itself. The proposal of permissive matrimony by no means insists upon this particular option; it merely insists that the option be available to those who want it. As has been indicated, conventional marriage would remain quite legal under the proposed scheme, and anyone who wished to (and could find a willing mate) would be perfectly free to commit matrimony. It seems only fair that those who prefer other alternatives should be equally free—again assuming that willing partners could be located.

One important question concerning alternative IV (and, to a lesser extent, some of the other alternatives as well) has to do with the fate of the offspring. The first point to remember is that as modern contraceptive methods become increasingly simple and reliable, the number of undesired pregnancies will become progressively smaller. A woman who suspects that her partner is a temporary one can quite readily take the proper precautions.

The second point has already been alluded to frequently in these pages, but should probably be recapitulated here. There is no sound evidence that children need to be brought up in our conventional family setting. Any re-evaluation of the presumed value of the husband-wife bond entails a corresponding re-evaluation of the parent-child bond. A *good* institution (i.e., one with adequate technological and human resources) may be expected to do at least as effective a job as a family in providing an environment conducive to optimal personality growth and happiness.

The purpose of institutions would be twofold: to care for children whose parents are unable or unwilling to care for them, and to care for children whose parents recognize the advantages of group care.[12] The source of funds would be, chiefly, the government—that is to say, the pockets of taxpayers. The financial burden, per individual, would be far less than that involved in bringing up a family.[13] Hardships to the children would be minimal—probably nonexistent. As Morison has predicted, it is the parents, rather than the children, who would be more likely to feel deprived if the influence of the family continues to decline; it is they who would have to look elsewhere for experiences that would make them feel important. The problem to be solved would be not so much parental deprivation as, to use Jenkins' term, "filial deprivation." How refreshing it would be for men and women to have to establish their feelings of self-esteem without using their children for this purpose!

Two additional questions now logically arise. First, if the state or community is ready to assume the expense, work, and responsibility for the bringing up of children, will there not be a further increase in our already burdensomely large population? Quite probably not. Few women will willingly go through the discomforts of pregnancy without the anticipation of keeping the child after birth.

A second possible consequence of community-rearing is the opposite of the first. If women are no longer motivated to have children, and if they have the freedom to prevent conception, how can society perpetuate itself? (It should be noted that this question indicates a general acceptance of the thesis being presented here, by presupposing that most individuals, given the choice, would choose not to bring up their own children. The question also presupposes that there is no such thing as a pre-maternal instinct.) If underpopulation ever becomes a problem, at least two solutions present themselves. First, does it not seem unfair that every able-bodied American male must be willing, if the need arises, to give two years of his life in order to fulfill a particular obligation of citizenship (compulsory military service), while females are entirely free of such responsibility? If, for whatever reason—and particularly if the reason is that the majority of individuals in the society freely choose for themselves a way of life that enhances their own happiness—the birth rate falls so low that social progress is threatened, then it would seem entirely proper to ask of our able-bodied women that they sacrifice, as a social obligation, a few months of comfort in order to bear a child. This is not a cruel, or inhuman, or callous, or unfair suggestion.[14] Pregnancy and childbirth are no longer the terrors they once were. Thanks to modern medical advances, and modern attitudes, pregnancy is not the incapacitating experience it was for our grandmothers. Present-day anesthetic techniques have greatly reduced the discomfort of childbirth; indeed, for many women fortunate enough to have obstetricians who are aware of the benefits of hypnosis or natural childbirth, it can be a downright enjoyable experience. Margaret Mead pointed out in 1949 that there are many parts of the world where women, even without benefit of anesthesia, feel no pain during childbirth, simply because they live in societies where pain is not expected. While it may be many years before our own society is sufficiently relaxed to have such attitudes, it is still a vast distortion to claim that compulsory motherhood would be tantamount to compulsory agony.

Another possible solution to the depopulation problem involves what Schlesinger has called "professional motherhood." Many women would undoubtedly welcome the opportunity to gain a steady livelihood by producing children. No one would be *forced* into this profession, and appropriate financial compensations and displays of social recognition could quite soon elevate motherhood to the rank of the other professions.[15] Women selecting this occupation would not, of course, be automatically burdened with the responsibilities of child-rearing. But those women who actively desire to rear children would be encouraged, after proper training, to work in the institutions. They would also be free to bring up in their own homes as many of their offspring as they could comfortably and usefully manage. Painstaking selection procedures would be necessary, both for the women and for their mates. (Obviously, these procedures would be required only for reproductive purposes. The professional child-producers would have as much freedom as anyone else in the choosing of recreational sexual partners.)

In short, the unlikely possibility of underpopulation does not constitute a serious obstacle to permissive matrimony. If most people prefer conventional marriage even in the absence of social pressures, then enough children will be produced. On the other hand, if widespread acceptance of marriage-free relationships should result in a serious decline in the birth-rate, then the measures indicated above could be implemented. At the risk of pointing out the obvious, it may be remarked that there is no immediate risk of underpopulation. One sociologist, Blake, has even recommended non-marriage (among other things) as a way of taking advantage of the "antinatalist tendencies that our present institutions have suppressed."

The reader should be reminded at this point that the institutionalization option is truly an option. And it should be obvious that institutionalization is not the only practicable alternative available to those who wish to avoid the dangers that may accompany conventional child-rearing practices. *Any* system that replaces our current emphasis on the intimate, exclusive bond between children and their parents is worthy of the most careful consideration. Communal upbringing has become increasingly popular and has already demonstrated its viability. In addition to the previously cited examples from Israel and the Oneida community, mention should be made of the Hutterites (a group of German ancestry, now settled in the Dakotas, Montana, and parts of Canada), whose system of early parent-child separation is associated with an extraordinarily low rate of childhood emotional disorders.[16]

Regardless of the directions that child-care may eventually take, it is appropriate to suggest here that society's responsibility for and to the next generation ought to extend beyond the making of provisions for the best available treatment. In view of the persistent threat of overpopulation and the deleterious effects of parental incompetence, it would be both rational and humane to require that all persons desiring to have children must have some minimal level of mental health and child-rearing skills. Society requires driver's licenses in order to prevent the unfit from endangering the lives of others. It is high time that children's rights were protected by the introduction of licensing for parents. Certainly this requirement makes more sense than our current insistence on marriage licenses. Irresponsible marriage is likely to harm, at most, two people: the self and the spouse. Irresponsible parenthood can irreparably damage a much larger number of victims. Caldwell has pointed out the irony that teachers must be certified because of the importance of correct treatment during the early years of life, while society seems to believe that anyone can be a good parent. The desirability and practicability of licensing parents have been spelled out in a recent article by McIntire. Obviously, great care would have to be taken in the procedures to screen out the unfit. In a matter of such great personal and social significance, an extremely permissive policy is called for, with licenses being denied only when there are extremely convincing reasons to believe that such an action is in the best interests of everyone concerned. For example, if both prospective parents are schizophrenic, or if they have a history of child abuse, their application should probably be denied. (As is the case with driver's licenses, the denial can be reversed as soon as clear evidence of competence is provided.)

The preceding discussion has focused on the possible effects of permissive matrimony on future generations. Let us turn now to a matter of more immediate concern, particularly with respect to those options that include multiple sexual partners. Many readers may feel repugnance at the very idea of mate-sharing. Possessiveness and jealousy are part of an especially vicious cycle: marriage and family life have been largely responsible, I suggest, for today's prevailing neurotic climate, with its pervasive insecurity, and it is precisely this climate that makes so difficult the acceptance of a different, healthier way of life. Nothing could be further removed from mental health than a man's being haunted by the fear that his wife will find someone with a penis larger or more satisfying than his own; or a woman's being desperately afraid that her husband will have a casual affair that will break up the marriage (the implication being, of course, that the reason her husband has been coming home day after day is neither spiritual, emotional, nor intellectual, but merely genital). Secretly aware that her personality is not attractive enough to keep any man interested for very long—marriage itself having stunted whatever remnants of a mature self had somehow survived the onslaught of her parents' neurotic needs—she has no choice but to defend the "ideal" of sexual fidelity, even at the cost of sacrificing her own chances for pleasant sexual variety. And her husband is on her side, too, unwilling to risk the possibility of coming out second best in a sexual comparison. Thus are the bonds of matrimony woven from the threads of emotional compulsions.

Individual opposition to a system that permits more than one sexual partner may have other roots as well, but these are usually less direct, being more closely tied to social and religious pressures. If there is such a thing as hell, nobody wants to be condemned to it; and most religions teach that there is no surer path to damnation than sexual "sin." It may not be out of place to remind the reader that the rigorous sexual restrictions from which he, as a God-fearing, society-fearing, body-fearing citizen is suffering are almost without exception the restrictions laid down by the "Elders" in the ancient religious communities—men so old that they had not had, we may assume, an urgent sex drive for several years; or else men who may well have been of dubious sexuality.[17] The answer to those who are afraid, either of genital competition or of eternal damnation, is simple; let them choose conventional monogamy. It should be clear that the proposed new system would not in any way infringe upon their legitimate rights.

We have seen, then, that permissive matrimony need have no adverse consequences on the adults concerned, their offspring, or society at large. But it is not enough to defend a projected social change by referring only to the damage it will not do. While it may be true that a society that does not coerce its members into matrimony would be a society without the many ill effects of marriage, the necessity remains of indicating the likely positive benefits of this proposal.

Would people be happier under such a system? They would certainly have a greater chance for sexual happiness, no longer restricted in their choice of bedmates by a set of artificial and outmoded social prohibitions. So long as the "official" morality persists, guilt feelings and fear of apprehension are likely accompaniments of nonmarital sex. Also, the sexual act is often abused in a restrictive society such as ours, being flaunted by many as a symbol of nonconformity. This sort of childishness would rapidly become obsolete in a system such as the one proposed here.

It would be naive to suppose that permissive matrimony would be characterized by total promiscuity. While there would be ample opportunity (except for those who opt for conventional monogamy) to enjoy a large number of sexual partners, many couples who discover an unusually gratifying condition of sexual compatibility might decide to stay together, for as long as the sexual compatibility continues. This temporarily stable relationship may seem, superficially, to resemble marriage; but it differs, in that it is contingent upon mutual satisfaction, is free of legal duties, and does not preclude what is now called infidelity.

Only rarely would these relationships become lifelong alliances. Transitory pairings are to be expected, because sexual compatibility is itself a transitory thing. Kinsey *et al.*[18] found that the age of maximum sexual activity for the average male in his sample was seventeen years, whereas the average female did not reach her peak of sexual activity until the age of about twenty-eight. While it is probable that a part of this age differential has a cultural explanation (sexual behavior in women being more suppressed by society than is the case for men, so that there is a longer "waiting period" for women), it still seems likely that a part of the age-gap is based on a developmental difference in the sex drives of the two sexes. We may theorize, on the basis of Kinsey's behavioral data, that the male's sex drive quickly develops to its maximum level (at age seventeen), and then begins a long, slow decline; the female's sex drive, on the other hand, takes a much longer time to develop. If a mating takes place when the boy and girl are both seventeen, the boy's desire is at its most intense, but the girl's is much less so. Under such conditions, reciprocity is unlikely. If the boy's requirements are met, the girl may feel exploited or used; and if the girl's needs determine the frequency of sexual behavior, then the boy may feel cheated or frustrated. Or consider another case: should the pairing begin when both partners are about twenty-three years old, all would go well for a while. The gradually subsiding sex drive of the male would be at approximately the same level as the gradually rising drive of the female, and mutual satisfaction would be probable. But what would happen if they stayed together for six years? The male's drive would be still lower, while his mate's would have reached its peak. With the woman desiring more frequent intercourse and the man less, a dangerous combination of dissatisfaction on the part of the woman and feelings of inadequacy on the part of the man would be the almost inevitable consequence.

This widespread mis-mating, which seems built into our present mating system, has an obvious remedy: a free selection of partners combined with a minimum of obstacles in the way of terminating relationships. Let us consider likely outcomes of this freedom of choice. Pairings between individuals of approximately equal drive states being optimally satisfying, we should expect that intercourse (or whatever other form of sexual behavior is chosen) between a seventeen-year-old male and a woman close to thirty would best suit the needs of each partner; such a pairing might well last a lifetime, because the two sex drives would be expected to decline at about the same rate. (In view of the higher mortality rates for men, this arrangement would also help to keep women involved in interpersonal relationships in the latter years of their lives.) Similarly, a girl of sixteen might be far happier with a man of fifty than with the passionate teen-ager she usually finds herself grappling with. When she becomes twenty-eight, her partner will be sixty-two and presumably less interested. She will then be ready for a teen-aged partner.[19]

This view of sexual relations meets its chief obstacle in existing social attitudes. We have learned stereotypes as to what constitutes sexual desirability. An eighteen-year-old girl is *supposed* to be more exciting than one ten years older. This attitude, and others like it, are nearly always based not on actual experience but on long-standing social conventions. What mother would allow her high-school son to have dates with a woman almost twice his age?[20] What woman would allow herself to be escorted in polite society by a lad of seventeen? Biologically meaningless prejudices against such pairings stand in the way. (It may be true that for some non-sexual kinds of relationships, a closer matching of ages would often be desirable. But the sexual partner certainly need not be the intellectual or athletic partner as well.)

Centuries ago, when relatively few people lived beyond the age of thirty, this problem of drive-discrepancy was probably not a very urgent one. But today, it may help to explain why sexual adjustment is such a rare occurrence in our society, both among the married and the unmarried.[21] ("Sexual adjustment" is obviously intended here to mean more than resignation to unfulfillment. Nor does it mean a series of "conquests" in which the prized outcome is neither orgasm nor closeness to another person, but merely victory.)

This discussion of drive-discrepancy can be easily misunderstood. I am not proposing that there be a monogamy-like relationship, terminating by mutual consent and followed by new semi-permanent relationships with new partners. While this sort of arrangement may frequently develop, it is also to be expected—and accepted—that there will be considerable "sleeping around" even during the period when the sex drives of the particular man and woman are most closely matched. Individuals get tired of the same food, the same weather, the same television programs, day after day and week after week. And yet, the desire for sexual variety remains largely unacknowledged (except in jokes and novels), and many of those who do satisfy these perfectly natural cravings—or even admit to having them—are punished either by social ostracism or by the pangs of conscience resulting from too many years of anti-sexual indoctrination.

As was pointed out above, it is possible that the discrepancy in frequency of sexual behavior of men and women at particular ages is culturally, rather than biologically, caused. But even if the cultural interpretation should prove correct, the plea for freedom of sexual choice would in no way be weakened. Do we want a set of social norms that results in many women being prevented from enjoying complete sexual fulfillment for more than fifteen years after puberty? At whatever age the sex drive is strongest, as well as at all other ages, the individual should have the right to unlimited sexual expression, provided only that his behavior does not infringe upon the rights of others. But as long as marriage and the monogamistic (or "monoga-mystic") ideal hold sway, pre-marital and extra-marital sex are regarded, almost automatically, as infringements—either on the rights of specific others or on the whole structure of public morality. Let it be noted, however, that (a) a system of permissive matrimony would not interfere with individual rights, because sexual freedom would not be an option to anyone who had pledged "fidelity" to a particular mate; and (b) the fact that 80% of the societies of the world permit multiple sexual partnerships strongly suggests that our society would not be risking ruination if it became equally tolerant.

For most people, conventional monogamy represents a major, and unnecessary, reduction in sexual pleasure. And if thwarted sexual desires are, as many authorities have long maintained, among the chief causes of emotional disturbance, then the message is glaringly clear. (There *are* those who maintain that there is virtually no limit to the amount of sexual variety that can be experienced between husband and wife. But how does this justify society's refusal to let a person have as many sexual partners as he wants?)

Sexual freedom is but one aspect of happiness that would be enhanced by a modification of existing marital traditions. An increasing emphasis on emotional independence, on honest human relationships, and on the full development of human potentialities may be expected, as the harmful effects of marriage—exploitation, parasitism, and a narrowing of personal horizons— gradually diminish. The advantages of taking child-rearing out of the generally inept (albeit well-meaning) hands of parents have already been outlined. In short, there is no reason to believe that men and women living in a society that does not emphasize marriage would be any less happy than the men and women of today, and the most rational prediction is that they would enjoy a considerably higher degree of happiness.

A final review of what would actually be involved under the proposed scheme may be useful here. Since personal freedom is at the root of this proposal, a set of rigid prescriptions is neither possible nor desirable. Marriage would continue to be a legal and socially accep-table institution, but non-marital and modified-marital relationships would be equally legal and socially accepta-ble. The duration of these relationships would be deter-mined by the individuals involved. There would be no limit as to the number of partners permitted. No obliga-tions of a financial nature would exist, unless specifically contracted. There would be no compulsory responsibility for child-rearing, and institutionalization would be com-pletely free of stigma, both for the child and for the parents who avail themselves of this alternative. A wom-an, man, couple, or group desiring to accept the responsibility of child-rearing would be free to do so, unless there is clear evidence of economic, physical, or psychological incapacity. Appropriate action would be taken in the case of parents who have refused to institu-tionalize a child and are then derelict in their care for him. The rights of all individuals would be legally pro-tected: no relationship involving an unwilling partner or one unable (because of feeble-mindedness, youth, etc.) to give intelligent consent would be permitted. Birth control information and equipment would, of course, be free and readily available.

The changes that permissive matrimony might engender in the social system would probably be quite small in number: tax laws and those governing inheritance would have to be modified; wage scales would shift so that women would receive the same pay as men for the same work; married men would no longer receive special economic consideration; housing patterns would change somewhat, with fewer large private dwellings being necessary. Changes such as these would not be difficult to implement and would neither destroy nor significantly alter those aspects of society that are worth preserving.

If relatively few people select options that do not require child-rearing, the number of child-care institutions currently in existence would probably be sufficient, although extensive modernization would be desirable. But if (as seems likely) large numbers of men and women decide upon relationships—such as child-free monogamy or temporary liaisons—that do not include child-care responsibilities, then additional institutions would have to be erected. Such a construction program would require tax increases, but this added out-of-pocket expenditure would be far less than the cost of bringing up a child at home. In the long run, another development may be anticipated: if the basic thesis of this book is correct, the devaluation of marriage in our society would be followed by a decrease in the incidence of mental illness and a consequent decrease in the need for mental institutions. At relatively small expense, the latter could be converted into child-care centers.

The caretaking centers would be operated in keeping with the best available knowledge concerning the needs of infants. Stimulation would be adequate and appropriate; nursing personnel would be carefully selected,[22] thoroughly trained, and well paid; and effective evaluative procedures would provide continual feedback with respect to the ongoing development of the infants. Thus, most of the factors responsible for the ill effects of institutionalization would be absent.

Children who remain in the institution, rather than being placed in foster or adoptive homes, would probably attend nearby schools. Alternatively, they could be educated within the institution by qualified teachers. In the latter case, there would be sufficient flexibility to incorporate new methods, subject matter, and educational philosophy, when these appear to be in the best interests of the child.[23] What values would these children be taught? Notwithstanding the fear of totalitarianism that emerges whenever group care is discussed, the most reasonable expectation is that the children would learn what used to be called—without cynicism—the American way of life: values, such as honesty, fair play, cooperation, and tolerance, that have been advocated so strongly but taught so poorly. It is to be supposed that the principles of ethical, productive and happy living will be learned more readily when children are free of the insecurities, engendered chiefly by parents, that ordinarily obstruct the internalization of these modes of thought. The children would also be exposed to the teachings of the various religions, along with the rationales for the atheistic and agnostic positions. Those who wish to embrace a particular religion would be perfectly free to do so.

As is true for most social reforms, the adoption of permissive matrimony would involve a transition period that would not be entirely free of difficulties. For example, many of the persons who at first appear eager to avoid or shake off the shackles of conventional marriage may find themselves surprised to learn that they are not *really* willing to part with their children at birth, or not *really* willing to share their mates with others. Likewise, many of those who find the idea of sexual freedom attractive might not, because of their early restrictive training, be able to adjust to a life in which non-marital sex is readily available. But we may assume that at least a fair number of volunteers *will* be able to overcome their earlier brainwashing. Whatever happens thereafter will depend largely on this nucleus.

The initial transitional period will constitute the most demanding test of the new system. Not only will the principles of permissive matrimony be put to the test of actual practice, but also the first practitioners will have to cope both with outsiders who castigate them and with internal residues of their own upbringing. This is the well-known "first generation" problem that besets all major revisions in social relations. In this particular case, there is every reason to believe that the problem can be overcome. The power of the family is growing progressively weaker. With the increasing tendency of teenagers to leave home (for college, the military, urban opportunities, and the like), the family's hold may weaken to such an extent that relatively free choice will be possible.[24]

The reader who finds this basic notion of individual freedom appealing should not shrug it off as too impractical. Agitation for more reasonable laws dealing with sexual behavior, serious discussions with friends, and intelligent scrutiny of the many forms of pro-marriage pressure and propaganda can go far toward creating a social environment in which permissive matrimony would be permitted to develop.

In a somewhat more activist way, people can cast off, to whatever extent they find comfortable, the many matrimonial trappings that trap us into the belief that there is something special about marriage. I am thinking here of such customs as newspaper engagement and marriage announcements, fancy weddings, the wife's assumption of the husband's name, and the wearing of wedding rings. As the "significance" of conventional marriage recedes, the acceptability of other options is likely to increase.

Individuals who are currently involved in non-marital relationships can add to the liberating trend by finding a middle course between the flagrant, antagonism-provoking showing off of their freedom, and the abject concealment that defines the relationship as a sordid one. The proper stance to take is probably an intensely private one: your marital status, like your politics and your religion, is your own business. If the private nature of human relationships were more widely acknowledged, we would eventually reach a point at which a person's social status would be independent of his marital status. At that point, the battle for permissive matrimony would be virtually won.

Finally, groups of like-minded individuals can accelerate the process of social acceptance of permissive matrimony by forming communities that would embody at least some of the ideas that have been outlined here. (Those who form such a community would be "like-minded" only in that they object to society's insistence upon conventional monogamy; some of them might, indeed, prefer monogamy, but within a context guaranteeing that their choice was made freely.) Implementation would be easiest in those states that have no legal prohibitions against "fornication" or non-marital "cohabitation." At present, according to Hefner, there are only two such states: Louisiana and Tennessee. Some pioneers may wish to explore the possibilities of establishing a community in another country.

Economic details would depend largely on the location of the community. In some cases, members of the group might have to seek or maintain employment in neighboring cities. On the other hand, the community might become economically self-supporting, gaining its livelihood from agricultural or other products. There is also the possibility of obtaining funds from wealthy benefactors or liberal foundations, but such windfalls cannot be realistically anticipated; besides, a fair assessment of the practicality of permissive matrimony would be difficult to make under such special circumstances. (This is not to say, of course, that financial support from interested parties should be automatically refused.)

Many experiments in social reform have failed because they attracted large numbers of immature or seriously disturbed people who manifested their problems in ways inimical to the best interests of the group. A screening procedure would, therefore, be desirable; persons failing to exhibit a satisfactory degree of stability should probably be denied membership. (This rather strict policy would be necessary only at first, while the community is in the process of developing itself and its public image. It may be assumed that membership would eventually be open to almost all applicants. Indeed, many disturbed individuals might well find living in the new community to be a therapeutic experience.) Even if there is an initial screening process, standards of admission cannot be unreasonably high. Not many specimens of perfect mental health are likely to emerge from the existing marriage-crazy society.

Many frustrated individuals, unable to find sexual mates in their own environment, might think of a non-marriage-oriented community as a paradise of partners who can be had for the asking. They will be disappointed. There is no reason to believe that selectivity would be abolished; and the repulsive, seriously disturbed man or woman is likely to be just as frustrated as in conventional society. With instant satisfaction not available, such persons would probably not remain in the community for very long.

Sexual behavior has received considerable attention in these pages, because sexual freedom, along with parent-free upbringing of children, constitutes the chief behavioral departures of the proposed system. But, as has already been indicated, life under the proposed new conditions would not be simply one long orgy. Rather, the rate of sexual behavior would probably turn out to be only slightly higher than is now the case. In our present restrictive society, sex has become a virtual obsession for large numbers of people. With social restrictions lifted, the role of sex in everday life would assume more reasonable proportions, being regarded merely as one among many forms of physical pleasure and one among many forms of social interaction. As such, the rate of sexual behavior would show an increase far less than would the rate of sexual enjoyment.

If a motto for the new system were necessary, "Freedom of sexual behavior" would be less accurate than "Freedom of social interaction." But even the latter is somewhat too narrow. Our marriage-made and marriage-mad society is so intent on linking eligible males with eligible females (while keeping "ineligibles" apart) that nearly every male-female social interaction, no matter how freely undertaken, is contaminated by its possible marital implications ("Are his intentions honorable?" "Does this relationship have a future?"). The person who socializes with "too many" members of the opposite sex may be as suspect as the one who socializes with too few.

Thus, the ultimate goal of permissive matrimony is simply the freedom to be oneself. That this goal of personal freedom happens to be highly congruent with the ideals of democracy leads to the prediction that the proposal should meet with less resistance in so-called free societies than in those more totalitarian. Future events may permit the testing of this prediction.

The arguments presented in these pages have been intended to indicate to the reader that permissive matrimony is a viable policy that does not deviate unduly from contemporary standards of interpersonal conduct.[25] A few words need to be said now to those who believe that the proposal is too conservative. Trenchant demands for the total abolition of marriage and the family are by no means new,[26] but they have become particularly vigorous in recent years because conventional matrimony is seen, by some, for example, Cantarow and associates, to be a major stumbling block in the path toward women's liberation. Although I sympathize fully with this view, I find myself unable to advocate the wholesale elimination of marriage at this time. One reason is a purely practical one: such a radical proposal has no chance of public acceptance, whereas the more evolutionary scheme proposed here may well receive support even from those who are personally opposed to some of its details.

There is a second, and more basic, reason for rejecting any demand for the immediate abolition of marriage. Such a demand is quite analogous to a demand for the immediate abolition of crutches (see p. 55). As long as there are people who are physically handicapped, there will be a need for crutches. And as long as there are people who are emotionally handicapped, there will be a need for marriage.[27]

Finally, there is the matter of individual freedom. Just as society has absolutely no right to force people into marriage, it has no right to prevent people from getting married. Readers who hold vehemently anti-marriage views may be somewhat consoled by the recognition that if marriage is as bad as they think it is, it will probably fade into obsolescence as more and more members of succeeding generations, progressively freer from the matrimonial imperative, select more liberating life-styles.

Permissive matrimony will not solve all of society's problems. There will still be crime, exploitation, and psychopathology. It is doubtless true that a thorough overhauling of many of our social institutions—economic, religious, and political—must be undertaken if human happiness and dignity are to have a fighting chance for survival. Marriage has been singled out for special attention in this book for several reasons. First, it may be the most influential of all social institutions, so that marital reforms are likely to have significant effects on the other institutions that need to be modified. A second, and related, point is that the child-rearing function of marriage provides the initial medium by which the other social institutions determine the lives of each successive generation. And third, individuals are more likely, through their own decision-making processes, to effect changes in marital patterns than they are to effect changes in the political, economic, or religious domains, which have proven to be relatively impermeable to individual action.

It is possible that a "perfect" society will never exist. But a vastly improved society *can* exist—if, and only if, enough dedicated men and women are able to envisage, and work toward, its actualization.

Afterword

I am singularly impressed with the fine job of presenting a sane and liberal viewpoint on marriage that Dr. Lawrence Casler has done, and done in such a succinct and lucid way, in *Is Marriage Necessary?*

By way of summation, I would like to consider his book chapter by chapter and try to make some salient comments on each. In Chapter I, "The Origins of Marriage," he thoroughly explores the reasons why monogamic mating probably arose, and concludes that when the satisfying of specific human needs no longer exists, which historically had been the raison d'etre for this kind of marriage, or when these needs "can be more efficiently satisfied outside of marriage, or when the needs themselves should be modified because they interfere with the full development of the individual and of society, then marriage becomes not only unnecessary but undesirable." This is a sound appraisal.

Marriage, obviously, has been created for the satisfaction of human desires—and some powerful desires (e.g., sex, love, companionship, partnership, and child-rearing) at that. But when enforced monogamy—as he clearly shows—tends to sabotage rather than to abet those desires, who wants it? Not, of course, that it always does. Many couples, even today, prefer monogamy. They appear to thrive better under its restrictions than they probably would under any other marital system and would logically remarry if the marriage ended. But a majority? I doubt it! Left with the undesirable alternatives they have today, such as socially disapproved free unions or open marriages, most married individuals might well select contemporary monogamy. But, as Dr. Casler shows (particularly in his last chapter) there are several possible sanctionable solutions. And if these are societally approved, monogamy may well become the worst alternative for most of the people most of the time.

In Chapter II, "Contemporary Marriage," Dr. Casler hauls modern monogamy over the coals and raises the possibility "that Western society is outgrowing marriage." Statistically, albeit surprisingly, this is not quite the case since during the last several decades the percentage of individuals marrying, and marrying at earlier ages, in the United States and in many other parts of the Western world, has actually risen. But Dr. Casler is not talking about marriage per se—that is, any form of marriage—rather he is addressing himself to enforced monogamy, and monogamy that is presumably kept the way it is "supposed" to be. Actually, as many recent works have shown, our so-called monogamic unions are really nothing of the sort. Technically, monogamy means once-in-a-lifetime mating, and precludes all divorce; what we have, instead, is one-at-a-time mating, or monogyny. This monogamous state, moreover, is very frequently broken by (a) premarital sex; (b) free love union; (c) adultery; (d) group sex, etc. Dr. Casler presents some evidence in this respect; and more evidence still, particularly about the nonmonogamous quality of contemporary marriage in the United States, is presented in many other recent works.*

*Among these are Morton Hunt's *The Affair* (New York: New American Library, 1971), Gerhard Neubeck's *Extramarital Relations* (Englewood Cliffs, N.J.: Prentice-Hall, 1969), Magar E. Magar's *Adultery and Its Incompatibility with Marriage* (Monona, Wisc.: Nefertite Publishers, 1972), and my own *Civilized Couple's Guide to Extramarital Adventure* (New York: Peter Wyden, 1972).

The facts are, therefore, that today marriage is only technically or theoretically monogamous; that it is more often than not monogynous or pluralist; and that it is becoming, in many different ways, more marital (that is, companionable and partnershiplike) but less exclusive. In this sense, Western society definitely seems to be outgrowing conventional marriage.

In Chapter III, "Child-bearing and Child-rearing" and Chapter IV, "Are Parents Necessary?" Dr. Casler has brilliantly exploded the myth that children naturally or biologically have a dire need for love or mothering and has shown that they very likely have, instead, strong predispositions to be physically and emotionally lacking if they do not receive adequate stimulation. Unfortunately, practically all modern psychology texts still persist in quoting Spitz and Ribble, whose authoritativeness Dr. Casler calls into serious question, and wrongly promote the Freudian-inspired thesis that unless children are reared by their own parents, especially their natural mothers, and are given profound and tender love by these parents, they have to grow up to be psychologically warped. Hogwash! By soundly ripping up this hypothesis in Chapter III and IV, Dr. Casler contributes a significant service. Careful reading of these chapter alone can provide the reader with material that is well worth the price of the book.

Although it is still stoutly believed by most psychologists and laymen that early environmental influences are crucial in the creation of emotional disturbances in humans and that maternal deprivation is particularly important in this respect, there is a mass of evidence disputing these theses. Significant research in this respect has been reported by Bettye Caldwell; Jane Oldman and Samuel Friedman; Arthur Novak and Ferdinand van der Veen; Jerome Kagan, William Sewell, and many other investigators. Dr. Casler showes that the entire subject of early childhood influence is at least a two-sided question and that it is by on means answered fully by the propagandistic writings of the staunch Freudians and monogamists.

In Chapter V, Casler cites chapter and verse on "The Destructivness of Marriage." Again, he really means the destructiveness of enforced and exclusive monogamic marriage. It is about this particular kind of mating that I think his conclusions aptly apply—namely, "its direct and indirect costs to society are enormous and insidious. For these reasons, marriage can be viewed as a social disease." Strong words, indeed, but about coercive monogamy, how true!

In his final chapter, Dr. Casler offers proposals and recommendations for the future. Here he espouses a system of "permissive matrimony," that includes these main options: (1) conventional monogamy; (2) modified monogamy; (3) nonmonogamous matrimony; and (4) nonmarital relationships. I cannot think of any decent or reasonable marital or nonmarital alternative that Dr. Casler has omitted here and I enthusiastically endorse his wide permissive range. Not that sex-love-marital permissiveness doesn't have its dangers and hassles. It definitely does! Those who try to effect it in their own lives, under our existing "monogamic" system, can easily run into difficulities. It is evident that Dr. Casler, from the standpoint of a social psychologist, recognizes the difficulties inherent in permissiveness but shows that these are hardly insurmountable. I decidedly concur.

Albert Ellis, Ph.D.

Notes

Chapter One

1. Supporters of the evolutionist position should remember, however, that evolution is an ongoing process. There is no justification for assuming that monogamy is the ultimate form of male-female relationships. Indeed, "in our present American culture, the only difference being that we practice 'serial polygamy' rather than the more orthodox kind" (Baber, 1953, p. 10). Also worthy of note is Chapman's comment that "as human beings become less selfish, polygamy . . . in an ennobled form, will become increasingly frequent" (quoted in H. Ellis, 1910, p. 501).

2. If there is any trend at all, it is in a non-monogamistic direction. The most highly evolved birds are not monogamous (Gilliard, 1963). One should also consider the possibility that monogamistic relationships arise from the attachment of the partners to the nest, rather than to one another (Kluijver, 1951). In any event, it is clear that those individuals who have maintained that "monogamy is for the birds" are only partially correct.

3. Lowie, 1933. In the same vein is Gerson's (1908) observation that peasant populations are more likely to be monogamous than are more industrialized groups with their "more versatile and sensitive tastes."

4. Malinowski, 1960, p. 940. Sumner and Keller

(1927) go so far as to assert that no human society has ever been sexually promiscuous.

5. "Function" is an exceedingly complex concept, with many subtle and intricate ramifications. (See Merton, 1957.) As used here, the term refers simply to whatever is presumed to be necessary in order for individuals or groups to attain their goals. "The principal objective [of functional analysis] is to exhibit the contribution which the behavioral pattern makes to the preservation or the development of the individual or the group in which it occurs" (Hempel, 1959, p. 278).

6. It is possible that all sexual regulations were, at first, merely extensions of the incest taboos that existed in polygamous societies. As the number of forbidden sexual relationships became ever greater because of the possibility thhat each member of the group might be related by blood to each other member, marriage might have been permitted only when this possibility had been convincingly negated. Non-marital liaisons within the group, being less subject to such careful inquiry, would become increasingly restricted.

7. Lindzey (1967) has offered fairly persuasive evidence for a genetic interpretation, but he neglects to consider the implications of contemporary developments in the field of contraception.

8. See Parsons and Bales, 1955, p. 399 and *passim*.

9. Italics added.

10. This is not to say that courtly love and courtly marriage were unrelated. It was fairly typical for the courtly lover to direct his passion at a woman already married to someone else.

11. Attributed to the Comtesse de Champagne's twelfth-century "Court of Love," cited in Beyle (Stendhal), 1947, p. 354. The contrary position, that marriage offers a basis from which love *can* be more freely given, also has its supporters and is reflected in the preceding comment by Ludlow. If this contention is valid at all, I would suggest that it is applicable primarily to

those who have difficulty relating to others in a spontaneous, non-routinized manner.

12. Briffault has been cited often in these pages, and it is only fair to point out that his credibility is not unimpeachable. Most of his conclusions were based on not-very-reliable reports from missionaries and early, relatively unsophisticated, anthropologists. Also, it is possible (as Malinowski and other critics have claimed) that his interpretations of anthropological field reports were sometimes far-fetched, and that he failed to take into account evidence contrary to his theoretical position. But these same criticisms can be (and have been) leveled against many of his critics as well. While we should not accept Briffault's statements as being automatically correct, we should likewise avoid the opposite error of automatically rejecting what he has to say. In these pages, Briffault is cited mainly when the present author has been unable to find reliable contradictory evidence. But no pretense is made to thorough acquaintance with the voluminous anthropological literature dealing with marriage and the family.

13. Briffault, 1927, vol. I, pp. 508–520; and vol. II, pp. 83 and 305. Professor S. Roark (personal communication) has informed me that at least some of these instances may be erroneous, reflecting Briffault's reliance on inadequate ethnographic sources. The reader should note that this question concerning the universality of marriage, while highly interesting, is only peripheral to the main theme of this book.

14. Some recent reports of the Nayar do not agree with Westermarck's account in all respects. (See Gough, 1959.) The controversy is based largely on how marriage is being defined. For our purposes, it may be sufficient to conclude that marriage, *as that term is usually understood*, did not occur among the Nayar. Closely related to—but not identical with—the question of the universality of marriage is the question of the universality of the family. Although "marriage" and "family" are

sometimes used interchangeably, the latter is usually used to describe the marital partners *plus* offspring and/or other closely related persons. Anthropologist Melford Spiro (1954) has asserted that the family does not exist in Israeli kibbutz society (also see p. 114). However, Spiro has subsequently (1960) expressed dissatisfaction with his earlier formulation.

15. For a more recent analysis, with a very similar conclusion, see Reiss, 1965.

16. It is important to note that "preferential marriage form" refers to what is most desirable (but not necessarily most frequent) in the particular society.

17. Bartlett, 1931, p. 159. *Cf*. Havelock Ellis's observation (1910, p. 495) that "man is an instinctively monogamous animal with a concomitant desire for sexual variation."

18. Murdock (*op. cit*.) concludes that (1) marriage exists only when the economic and the sexual are combined in one relationship, and (2) this combination occurs only in marriage.

19. Dissent from this common-sense point of view exists but is unconvincing. One writer (Greenwood, 1956, p. 46) asserts that "rather than being an institution that was created by man, it seems more likely that man and the family have always, of necessity and in virtue of natural law, been co-existent and institutionalized."

Chapter Two

1. Kinsey, Pomeroy, & Martin, 1948; Kinsey, Pomeroy, Martin, & Gebhard, 1953.

2. See, for example, Himelhoch & Fava (Eds.), 1955, especially Chapters IV and VII.

3. This figure rises to approximately 83% for females in the lower socio-economic classes (Kinsey *et al*., 1953). Although Kinsey's data are no longer new, they probably are still valid. While there may have been a

"sexual revolution" in *attitudes*, the percentage of individuals engaging in non-marital sexual *behavior* has remained fairly stable (see Smigel & Seiden, 1968). Contrary impressions may have arisen because people are less secretive about their sex lives than they used to be.

4. The irreverent might argue that what the missionaries actually contributed was a high degree of "syphilization."

5. "On Some Verses of Virgil" (orig. pub., 1585–1588), p. 646 in the Frame edition.

6. See Havighurst, 1948, p. 1194.

7. Briffault, 1931, p. 434. Briffault here contradicts a statement published by him one year earlier: "Cultural history shows that the amount of trouble caused by sex is in almost exact reverse proportion to the cultural restrictions to which it is subjected" (1930, p. 693). Another commentator (Lewinsohn, 1958) has countered the usual historical position with respect to Rome, concluding that "sexual abstinence did more than excess to bring about the downfall of Rome" (p. 101).

8. G. B. Shaw was one of the first to discuss the concept of marriage-as-prostitution: "Whilst the man defends marriage because he is really defending his pleasures, the woman is even more vehement on the same side because she is defending her only means of livelihood. . . . The difference between marriage and prostitution [is] the difference between Trade Unionism and unorganized casual labor" (1971, pp. 500–501, orig. pub., 1911). The objection may be made that these days, it is not so much her sexual services as her domestic services (cleaning, cooking, babysitting) that the woman is selling. Likewise, economic rewards are not the only kind traded off by the husband. He is also in a position to supply "respectability" (Eckland, 1968). The basic point, of course, remains the same: marriage often reduces a woman to a condition of servitude (see p. 126).

9. Economic considerations have even led some com-

mentators to the opposite conclusion, that the best hope for our society and its members would be the elimination, not the perpetuation, of our current family structure. See Calverton, 1928; and Wittles, 1930.

10. This phenomenon has been repeatedly documented. The reader is referred, in particular, to the classic study by Burgess and Wallin (1953). It should be stressed here that the mutual attraction of persons with *similar* beliefs and values in no way contradicts the theory that attraction may also be based on the *complementarity* of psychological characteristics, such as dominance and submission, as postulated by Winch (see Winch, Ktsanes, & Ktsanes, 1954). Also worth noting here is the distinction between the insecure seeking of confirmation and the more rational desire for communality of interests within a relationship.

11. This notion is congruent with, but not dependent upon, Freud's (1922) explanation of love in terms of "aim-inhibited sex."

12. According to a folk-saying of unknown origin, the way to a woman's genitals is through her heart, while the way to a man's heart is through his genitals.

13. Boissier de Sauvages, quoted in H. Ellis, 1910, p. 513. And Greenfield (1965, p. 375) has described it as "institutionalized irrationality."

14. The title of an article by the present author, "This Thing Called Love is Pathological" (1969), was an editorial addition that does not reflect my position. For the most complete account of this position, see Casler, 1973.

15. Birdwhistell, 1966, p. 212. In the same passage, the point is made that it is equally impossible for parents to meet all the needs of their children.

16. Thamm, unpublished manuscript. There is an anonymous saying (quoted in Waller & Hill, 1951, p. 255) that seems to express the same idea after subjecting it to a 180-degree rotation: "Marriage is the remedy for the disease of love." (See also Montaigne, *op. cit.*, p. 649.) Both of these pronouncements are, of course, var-

iations on the well-established theme that familiarity breeds contempt.

17. "Marrying and having children were considered sacred with the Greeks, and most essential patriotic duties [Kelsen, 1942, p. 30]."

18. *Cf*. Hitler's dictum that "the German girl is a State Subject and only becomes a State Citizen when she marries" (1939, p. 659).

19. The other side of the coin, the pressure *for* children after marriage, has been briefly mentioned in Chapter I and will be discussed further in Chapter III.

20. Christensen, 1960. These statistics probably do not apply to the many couples who begin a non-marital relationship with the agreement that the birth of a child will not change their relationship but will merely provide a situation in which marriage becomes necessary in order to legitimize the child. It is not realistic to regard such marriages as of the "shot-gun" variety.

21. *Book of Common Prayer*, "The Form of Solemnization of Matrimony."

22. 1 Corinthians 7. St. Augustine later offered the following somewhat milder version: "Marriage and fornication are not two evils whereof the second is worse, but marriage and continence are two goods whereof the second is better" (1956, pp. 402–403).

23. For one segment of the population, the emphasis on the sanctity of marriage was initially quite appealing; indeed, the Church's insistence on the indissolubility of marriage "contributed appreciably to the high rate of conversions to Christianity among women" (Lewinsohn, 1958, p. 92).

24. "He who abstains from marrying is guilty of bloodshed, diminishes the image of God, and causes the divine presence to withdraw from Israel" (*Shulhan' Arukh* [Jewish Code of Laws]: *Even hafzer*, 1:1).

25. For documentation of these statements, see *Encyclopedia Judaica*, Vol. 14, pp. 1206–1207 (Macmillan, 1971). It should be made clear that most adherents

of contemporary Judaism probably have no knowledge of these dicta and are influenced by them quite indirectly, if at all.

26. Cited by Montaigne, 1967, p. 147.

27. *Statesman*, stanza 271. According to both Gregory of Nyssa and John of Damascus, "If Adam had preserved his obedience to the creator, he would have lived forever in a state of virgin purity, and some harmless mode of vegetation would have peopled paradise with a race of innocent and immortal beings [May, 1931, p. 29]."

28. Greenwald (1970) has made the interesting observation that it would be quite consistent for the various religions to withdraw their support from state-authorized marriage, in order to strengthen their own power in matters of marriage and divorce.

29. "People who reject marriage are neurotics" (Bergler, 1958, p. 249).

30. Interestingly, after an apologia for marriage on the grounds that people need structure, the O' Neills proceed to endorse a type of marital relationship considerably less structured than many of the non-marital arrangements of which they disapprove. For further discussion of "open marriage," see p. 151.

31. Universal Declaration of Human Rights, Article 16, Section 3: "The family is the natural and fundamental group unit of society..." (United Nations, 1949, p. 536). Among innumerable other expressions of this idea, the following is a typical example: "The family is too indispensable a unit of social structure and too necessary a means for the transmission of culture to the oncoming generation to be allowed to fall apart" (Blood, 1960, p. 211). A major obstacle to the intelligent re-evaluation of marriage as an institution is that statements such as this are cited or reprinted in college texts (see, for example, Hadden & Borgatta, 1969), with opposing viewpoints receiving little or no attention. Moore (1958) reacts to such pronouncements as follows: "I have the uncomfortable

feeling that the authors...are doing little more than projecting certain middle-class hopes and ideals onto a refractory reality. If they just looked a little more carefully at what was going on around them, I think they might come to different conclusions" (p. 161).

Chapter Three

1. Groves, 1941, p. 516. There has also been a counter-tendency: "Childlessness became a social virtue, already established in the Unted States by 1700" (Zimmerman, 1947, p. 157). But this can best be viewed as an undercurrent that never affected more than a small segment of the population.

2. But see Hoffman & Wyatt, 1961.

3. In a recent study by the present author (1970), these exploitative factors were quite apparent.

4. Clarkson, *et al.* 1970. It should be noted that the cause-effect relationship here is by no means clear. Does low self-concept result in the desire for many children, or do the difficulties of taking care of many children result in a lowering of the self-concept, or do large families and low self-concepts both owe their origins to membership in the lower socio-economic strata? In support of the first of these possibilities, Helene Deutsch (1951) has writtten that some women may become pregnant because they are seeking "a kind of vacation from difficult endeavors and from feelings of inferiority" (p. 16).

5. In many—probably most—cases, we may expect these motives to be denied by their possessors. "People desire children for reasons largely unknown to themselves" (Winch, 1950, p. 314).

6. "I have never thought that to be without children was a want that should make life less complete and less contented" (Montaigne, "Of Vanity, " 1967, p. 764).

7. See Mead, 1949, p. 48; and Bergler & Roheim, 1946.

8. Boffey, 1970. Health insurance plans reduce the out-of-pocket expenses even further—sometimes to less than one dollar.

9. For two studies pointing in this direction, see Christensen & Philbrick, 1952; and Landis, Poffenberger, & Poffenberger, 1950.

10. For an excellent analysis of the variables involved, see Lehrman, 1961.

11. Sumner & Keller, 1927. It should be obvious, nevertheless, that although breast feeding may be *sufficient* for the establishment of a mother-child bond, it is not *necessary* for this purpose. Research with rats has revealed that maternal behavior is not dependent upon mammary gland engorgement (Moltz, Geller, & Levin, 1967).

12. The society maintained itself by recruiting members from the outside.

13. Richard Rabkin, personal communication.

14. On the other hand, Malinowski (1930) has written that in a tribe where there are such practices as infanticide or frequent adoption, "the natural innate tendencies of maternal love may become rebelliously subservient to custom and tribal law, but they are never completely stifled or obliterated [p. 118]." No evidence exists in support of this assertion.

15. Reiss (1965) has convincingly argued that "nurturant socialization" is the *only* function universally fulfilled by nuclear families. See, also, Levy & Fallers, 1959.

Chapter Four

1. See, for example, Bowlby, 1960, p. 34. And even the separations that begin after the age of six months are not invariably traumatic (Wolins, 1970).

2. There is, for example, the "congenital neurolabile constitution" described by Örsten and Mattson (1955). And Stevenson (1948) reports that some ill ef-

fects of adverse conditions during childbirth may not manifest themselves until the child is four years old, or even older.

3. Many of these conditions have been found to persist at least until the age of seven years. See Takkunen, Frisk, & Holmström, 1965. While the explanation for these serious consequences of prematurity remains in doubt, two theories deserve careful attention. First, there is the paucity of sensory stimulation within the incubator (see later pages of this chapter). Second, there is the possibility of brain damage resulting from asphyxia (Windle, 1969).

4. For other relevant research on the effects of mother's milk, see Hofer, 1970.

5. It should be pointed out that this author paints a somewhat more attractive picture of foster parents than Glaser does. This discrepancy may reflect the fact that Babcock obtained her information from case workers whom the foster parents were very likely trying to impress.

6. Bowlby, *et al.*, 1956, p. 211. This partial disavowal has been largely ignored by other writers in the field. "We run a risk of creating new myths of our own which linger on even after their creators have modified or renounced their claims'; we must, for instance, expect much time to pass before the extensive public which finds in maternal separation an easy explanation of problem behavior becomes aware of the second thoughts voiced by Bowlby and his colleagues" (Wootton, 1959, p. 328). Wootton has also characterized Bowlby's neglect of genetic factors as "incredibly naive" (*ibid.*, p. 147).

7. It omits the older, more fragmentary reports (included in Casler, 1968), as well as those that are inconclusive (such as that by Tizard & Tizard, 1967, whose findings sometimes favor the institutionalized group and sometimes favor the family-reared controls).

8. *Cf.* the comment that "multiple mothering need not be seen as a traumatizing experience...but rather

as an inoculation against social shyness and fear" (J. McV. Hunt, 1960, p. 163). Another investigator has suggested that "the larger child and adult population in an institutional environment may lead the infant to be precocious socially, mature in his practical judgments, and to have some forms of emotional control prematurely developed" (Bridges, cited by Brody, 1956, p. 77). The statement is expressed rather negatively, as if the usual rate of development were necessarily the best.

9. See also Wootton's (1959) reinterpretation of the earlier data.

10. A similar belief had been expressed earlier by Wootton (1959, p. 155): "As much good may be done by running the institutions better as by leaving the children in their homes."

11. "Sensory" and "perceptual" are occasionally used interchangeably, but it is more accurate to reserve the latter term for the organization or interpretation of sensory experience. Thus, we may have the *sensation* of a red, white, and blue stimulus, but we would *perceive* an American flag. See also Kubzansky and Leiderman, 1961.

12. One may note here that childhood autism, one of the more serious emotional disorders of early childhood, has been successfully treated by means of "massage therapy" (Waal, 1955). See also Schopler (1965).

13. A report of preliminary research by Solkoff *et al.* (1969) suggests that the motoric retardation frequently found in premature babies (see p. 82) may be remediable by supplementary handling.

14. Harlow, 1958, p. 684. Quite strikingly, Karl Bühler (1919) had reported much earlier that crying infants could be effectively quieted with a soft cushion or a hot water bottle. Harlow's data can be interpreted in more than one way, and a more recent report from his laboratory (Harlow & Harlow, 1966) includes the statement that the security provided by the cloth surrogate is *less* than that provided by the real mother.

15. There is more to say about Harlow's findings. See p. 197.

16. The kinds of experience described in this paragraph probably involve a combination of kinesthetic and vestibular sensations. In the interests of simplicity, the two types of stimulation are here treated as one.

17. Without alertness to the outside world, learning is greatly impeded (see p. 109). The low IQs of institutionalized infants may thus be nothing more than the result of vestibular and other forms of deprivation.

18. For an interesting discussion of still other possible consequences of movement restraint, see Wunderlich, 1967. Also worthy of consideration is the suggestion by Brenneman (1932) that the middle-ear infections found in the majority of the institutionalized infants whom he studied may have been caused by the vomitus that could not be ejected by the supine infants. Moreover, a high correlation has been found between head-banging—a frequent consequence of prolonged immobility—and infections of the middle ear (de Lissovoy, 1963). Perhaps it is time to reject the contention by Gelinier-Ortigues & Aubry (1955) that infections of this kind result from maternal deprivation. (For a discussion of possible side-effects of infections, see p. 84).

19. According to Fischer (1958, p. 372), "It is well known than even three-to-four-month-olds often protest violently against the supine position, and calm down when they are held or propped up in a sitting position, because this allows a more extended and gratifying field of vision." The institution studied by Dennis & Najarian had a number of other deficiencies. Like those described by Spitz and others, it had a child-caretaker ratio of approximately 10:1, a far cry from the 4:1 ratio believed (see Bertoye, 1957) to be optimal.

20. Robson (1967) has stressed the developmental importance of eye-to-eye contact, but there is no evidence that maternal eyes are more able to foster growth than are the eyes of impersonal caretakers.

21. "The child can obviously develop a meaningful vocabulary only to the extent that he has had the opportunity to hear the spoken word" (McKinney & Keele, 1963, p. 561).

22. Similarly, Walters and Parke (1965) contend that attachments to people are based on their ability to provide stimulation.

23. The "European manner" is, of course, what is currently employed in the vast majority of U. S. families and U. S. institutions.

24. For a summary of these, see White, 1969.

25. See Solomon *et al.* (Eds.), 1961. Similar symptoms have been reported for polio patients confined to respirators (Mendelson, Solomon, & Lindemann, 1958), and for patients immobilized for treatment of fractures and for other medical reasons (Meyer, Greifenstein, & Devault, 1959).

26. See Smolen, 1965. *Cf.* this comment by Lessac and Solomon (1969, p. 14): "Behavioral development may not merely be retarded by isolation, it may be distorted."

27. On the other hand, the learning abilities of rhesus monkeys appear to be unimpaired by early isolation (Angermeier, Phelps, & Reynolds, 1967).

28. It is important to avoid generalizing from the rhesus monkey to other varieties of monkey. See p. 107.

29. Experiments have revealed that babies whose smiling is not rewarded by appropriate environmental stimulation will show marked reductions in frequency of smiling (Brackbill, 1958). And we learn from Kistyakovskaya (1965) that "smiling and other positive emotional responses are elicited mainly by prolonged visual and auditory stimuli that need not be people."

30. Robertson (1962) relates thumb-sucking specifically to absence of verbal stimulation.

31. *Cf.* the report that rats deprived of handling are very likely to develop dermatitis (Hatch *et al.*, 1963). Premature children, who constitute a disproportionately

large segment of most institutionalized populations (see p. 82), are known to have particularly sensitive skins (Tyson, 1946).

32. For an account of more recent research, see Beck, Dustman, & Sakai, 1969.

33. Racamier, 1953, and Rosenzweig *et al.*, 1968, provide more detailed descriptions of the available evidence.

34. "From babies without love, they become adults full of hate." See also Stekel, 1930.

35. This is not to say that *any* institution will suffice. If a child's formative years are spent in an atmosphere of cruelty or neglect, he may never develop the confidence in himself and in his social environment that will enable him to relate freely and warmly to other people.

36. With no unequivocal evidence for love among lower animals, with entire societies devoid of what we would call love, and with no organic basis yet discovered, the instinctive basis for love—or for the need thereof—is extremely doubtful (see Casler, 1973). "The proposition that the human infant has certain innate needs for social stimuli (e.g., mothering, love) appears only remotely useful heuristically" (Gewirtz, 1966, p. 34). But while the learning hypothesis seems clearly preferable, this does not mean that the requisite learning takes place in infancy.

37. Before concluding this part of the discussion, it is worth noting that perceptual deprivation may obscure other, more basic deficiencies. "Only part of the apathy noted in maternally deprived infants may stem from under-stimulation; simple starvation may also be a factor" (Whitten, Pettit, & Fischhoff, 1969, p. 1682).

38. Church, 1926. This is not to imply that Oneida was entirely free of internal dissension. But the fact remains that the society failed because of external pressures.

39. Irvine, 1952. For an excellent account of changes that have been taking place on kibbutzim, see Irvine, 1966.

Chapter Five

1. Montaigne reports that when Socrates was asked which was preferable, to take or not to take a wife, he replied, "Whichever a man does, he will repent it" ("On Some Verses of Virgil," p. 649 in the Frame [1967] translation; orig. pub., 1585–1588).

2. Bell, 1962. Likewise, society's emphasis on the joys of, or necessity for, having children may cause many childless men and women to feel somehow inadequate or incomplete.

3. *op. cit.*, p. 473. Ellis also compares marriage to a mousetrap—easy to get into, but difficult to get out of (p. 504). There are innumerable other expressions, from various sources, of the same general idea. Montaigne, for example, likens marriage to a birdcage, in which "the birds outside despair of getting in and those inside are equally anxious to get out" (*op. cit.*, p. 647). Elsewhere, Montaigne (*ibid.*, p. 137) comments that marriage is "a bargain to which only the entrance is free—its continuance being constrained and forced, depending otherwise than on our will—and a bargain ordinarily made for other ends." Or, as Leringer (1965, p. 20) has put it, "marital strength is a function of bars as well as bonds." These days, for the purpose of brevity, we might prefer to speak of the progression from dating to mating to hating, or from telephone ring to wedding ring to suffering.

4. On the other hand, Hunt (1959) and Brown (1966) report that approximately 75% of married people are happily married. (Note that this finding does not necessarily mean that 75% of marriages are happy marriages, nor that the happily married will remain happily married, nor does it take into account the fact that surveys of married couples do not include persons who were formerly married but unhappily so.

5. Pineo, 1961. *Cf.* Bertrand Russell's observation (1957, p. 137) that "very few marriages after the first

few years are happy." Although most studies do indicate
that older people are generally less happy than younger
people, one report concludes that there is *no* strong
relationship between self-reported happiness and
chronological age (Kuhlen, 1959). Nevertheless, Pineo's
finding needs to be viewed with caution, Cross-sectional
research by H. Feldman (unpub.) indicates that marital
happiness does decline during the course of the marriage but shows an increase toward the end.

6. Burgess and Wallin, 1953. This is not to say that
the emotional dependency is caused by the happy marriage; perhaps it is the other way around, with emotional
dependency being necessary for a happy marriage. Also
worthy of note is the finding, by Dyer & Luckey (1961),
of *no* relationship between personality scores and marital happiness scores. The major obstacle preventing a
clear-cut conclusion on this issue is the lack of precise
measuring instruments for either personality or marital
happiness.

7. This discussion parallels the observations made earlier concerning the need for love. See p. 123. The point
to be borne in mind is that we can deeply enjoy the
experience of sharing many aspects of our lives, without
going so far as to be able to enjoy an experience *only*
when it is shared. Contrary to the lyrics of a predictably
popular song, people who need people are *not* the
luckiest people in the world.

8. In a collection of articles by David Mace, this yoke
was referred to as the "altar halter" (Mace, personal
communication, 1973).

9. Justice Jacob Panken, cited in de Lys, 1958, p. 32.

10. Schooley (1936) was among the first to report this
phenomenon. There have been occasional contradictory
findings. See Kelly, 1955.

11. de Beauvoir, 1961, p. 450. *Cf.* her comment,
concerning the Greece of Demosthenes' day, that "marriage, intended to enslave women, was also a ball and
chain for man" (p. 84), and Ambrose Bierce's definition

of marriage as "a community consisting of a master, a mistress, and two slaves, making in all, two" (p. 86). Friedrich Engels (1902) pointed out that the word *familia* is derived from *famulus*, meaning "domestic slave." See also Briffault, 1927, Vol. II, p. 336.

12. For a review of recent studies, see Hicks and Platt, 1970. It is difficult to reconcile these findings with the assertion that "by and large, a 'good' marriage, from the point of view of the personality of the participants, is likely to be one with children; the functions as parents reinforce the functions in relation to each other as spouses" (Parsons & Bales, 1955, p. 21).

13. Booth, 1929, p. 67. *Cf.* Hitler's (1939, p. 621) declaration that "the aim of feminine education is inevitably to be the future mother," and the statement, by Goebbels (quoted in Millett, 1970, p. 165), that "the outstanding and highest calling of woman is always that of wife and mother, and it would be unthinkable misfortune if we allowed ourselves to be turned from this point of view."

14. Study by B. Levinson, reported in *New York Times*, April 17, 1960, p. 72.

15. Ostwald & Regan, 1957, p. 153. "Puerperal insanity" was, at one time, a standard diagnostic category (see Jacobs, 1943).

16. LeMasters, 1957. It should be pointed out that most of these crises are of a temporary nature. Some readers might even argue that these stresses are of value, serving to "mature" the parents. There is, however, no evidence that this the case. Indeed, Feldman's (*op. cit.*) finding that subsequent births are sometimes even more psychologically stressful for the parents than was the birth of the first child points in the opposite direction. (See also p. 69)

17. *ibid.*, p. 122. For another forceful book-length indictment of conventional motherhood, see J. C. Rheingold, 1967.

18. Reed, 1929., p. 43. In the next chapter, this sug-

gestion will be expanded to include prospective fathers as well.

19. Peshkin, 1930. See, too, Shaw's (1971) recommendation that the divorce laws be broadened to permit children to obtain divorces from their parents.

20. Rollin, 1970. Child abuse is not, of course, a new phenomenon. The Factory Acts of the nineteenth century were "aimed to protect the child not only against his employer but also against his parents, who might be willing to connive at his exploitation" (Reed, 1929, p. 94).

21. A number of clinical studies and illustrative case histories are included in a collection of readings in abnormal psychology by Rabkin & Carr (1967).

22. On the other hand, we have an unsupported contention by Sait (1938, p. 493) that "the weakening or elimination of ["the individual ties between parents and children"] might....be detrimental to the development of independent thinking."

23. It is only fair to remind the reader that Freud also claimed that mental health is possible only if the Oedipus complex is successfully resolved. Thus, a Freudian would argue that mental health would be impossible if there were no Oedipus complex to resolve. If this position were valid, all the world's societies that do not have the nuclear family structure would be afflicted with entire populations lacking in mental health. Such a conclusion appears to be extremely ethnocentric.

24. Howe, 1931, p. 368. *Cf.* the suggestion by House (1929) that the Oedipus complex may stem from the passionate need of frustrated mothers for their sons.

25. Dührssen, 1958. Not all comparisons favored the institutionalized children, who were found to be clumsier and displayed greater apathy. The description of this particular institution indicates that it was a grossly inadequate one.

26. Landis, cited by de Lys, *op. cit.*, p. 91. Also see Watson, 1930; and the section on divorce in Neill, 1960.

27. A similar point has been made by Goode (1964, p. 80). The statement by Espinas (1878), that Western family structure hampers social evolution because family cohesiveness renders less likely the formation of new societies, is no less true now than when it was written almost a century ago. There seems to be no justification for Sait's (1938) prediction that a weakening of familial ties would *impede* social progress.

28. 1946, p. 44. Reference will be made in the next chapter to the idea that one reason the Soviet Union abandoned its liberal post-Revolution marital policies was that governmental control of individuals was deemed easier when transmitted via the family. If true, this point runs counter to the frequently expressed fear that institutional upbringing is dangerous because governmental brainwashing can take place more readily than in family settings.

29. 1954, p. 477. This observation is based on a cultural-learning hypothesis. The same conclusion emerges from a functional analysis of the social structure. See Parsons, 1954; and Reiss, 1965.

30. Testimony of Lincoln and Alice Day, U. S. House of Representatives, 1969, p. 86.

31. The reader should note, too, that the relationship between marital status and suicide is reversed for those under the age of 25 (Dublin, 1963).

32. She comments, further, that marriage is a "surviving relic of dead ways of life" (pp. 429-430).

33. This sentiment is an ancient one. When Thales (640–546 B.C.) was young, he asserted that it was not yet time to marry; when he became older, he said that the time for marriage had passed (Montaigne, 1967, p. 282).

34. This statement is based on the results of the most thorough epidemiological study to date (Srole *et al.*, 1962), which revealed imperfect mental health in 80% of the individuals surveyed. Inasmuch as this study con-

centrated on an urban population, a significantly lower figure is presented here, because of the (unlikely) possibility that people in non-urban areas are psychologically healthier than those residing in large cities. That this latter assumption is probably erroneous is suggested by the work of Goldhamer & Marshall (1953).

Chapter Six

1. Students of the history of cultural anthropology will recognize similarities between this description of modified monogamy and the "syndyasmian" family that Lewis Morgan (1878) proposed as an early stage in the evolution of marriage.

2. Case of State *v*. Armstrong, cited by Ploscowe, 1962, pp. 139–140.

3. David Sills (Population Council Seminar, cited by Fawcett, 1971) has persuasively urged that the term "child-free" is preferable to the term "childless." Although Sills was referring specifically to strategies for population control, his point is equally pertinent in the present context. "Childless" implies incapacity or deprivation; "child-free," on the other hand, has connotations of a much more positive kind.

4. Lindsey & Evans, 1927. *Cf.* the proposal, offered as a partial solution to the population problem, that there be two types of marriage, one of them child-free and easily terminable, and the other licensed for children and intended to be stable (Meier, 1959).

5. For a description and analysis of Soviet marital reforms, see Millett, 1970; and Moore, 1958. The relatively brief experiment did yield dividends. "Whatever else can be said about the Russian state's 'taking over' the traditional functions of the family, it is...clear that family

members reaped definite benefits" (Kenkel, 1960, p. 145). These benefits, Kenkel goes on to say, included reductions in "sickness, poverty, and suffering."

6. But consider Ellis' (1910, p. 497) interesting observation that polygyny permits "the most vigorous and successful members of a community to have the largest number of mates and so to transmit their own superior qualities." (The same point would presumably apply to polyandry as well.) A notable attempt in this direction was the "Mittgarbund" movement in Germany (de La-Pouge, 1908), in which polygyny and community-controlled procreation were practiced with the express goal of social improvement. Unfortunately, this appears to have been a rather small-scale experiment, and the results have not been reported in detail.

7. Hart & Hart, 1941, p. 16. These favorable conditions may not be correctly attributable to the modified family system at all, but rather to the extremely religious orientation of the community, or to still other socio-psychological factors. For an excellent account of the Oneida experiment, see Leslie, 1967.

8. We must bear in mind, however, that many communes are defined by their members as intentionally transitory, so that early dissolution is not necessarily a sign of failure.

9. Albert Ellis has recently (1970) written an excellent critical discussion of group marriage.

10. The same point can be made, of course, with respect to monogamous pairings that do not involve sexual exclusivity.

11. See Shaw, 1971; and Blood, 1960.

12. Note the never fully realized promise of the Soviet Revolution; the state was intended to "assume charge of the children, signifying not that they would be *taken*

away from their parents, but that they would not be *abandoned* to them" (de Beauvoir, 1961, p. 682, italics in original).

13. It is easy to say that the government will subsidize child-care institutions, but can this be viewed as a realistic possibility? A few years ago, the answer would probably have been negative. But the significant progress that is now apparent in the establishing of publicly supported day-care centers provides reason for optimism. And although supplementary private funding may well be necessary, federally financed demonstration projects are by no means out of the question.

14. Nor is it a new suggestion. As early as 1909, Ellen Key was advocating a year of compulsory service for women, including instruction in child care.

15. See Russell, 1930, pp. 22–23. Several decades ago, social reformer Sidney Webb had advocated social rewards for motherhood. (See H. Ellis, 1910, p. 629.)

16. Eaton & Weil, 1955. The strict religiosity of this group may also be related to the reported findings. Other experiments in parent-child separation, such as Fruitlands and the Army of Industry (Holloway, 1951), and Point Loma (Baker, 1907), do not provide us with very useful information. Generally speaking, they did not last long, for reasons unrelated to child-rearing procedures. These experiments do provide precedents of a sort, and a careful study of their mishaps may help future pioneers to avoid making the same mistakes.

17. "The vigorous men of later periods have had to do their best to live up to an outlook on life belonging to diseased, weary, disillusioned men who had lost all sense of biological values" (Russell, 1957, p. 43). A similar observation has been made by Lewinsohn (1958, p. 105): "It will perhaps be objected that the life of most

founders of religions was sexually abnormal. This is true and is why most religious sex-laws are so wrong-headed." See also Cohen, 1919.

18. 1953, p. 715. See also Christensen & Gagnon, 1965.

19. And what happens to the 62-year-old men? Those who still desire a companion will find many older women available. Although, as was just stated, many of these women may already be involved in fairly permanent alliances, there will probably still be a surplus of women in the older age bracket. (Also, it should be remembered that we are no longer talking about an exclusively monogamous system.)

20. A part of this parental resistance may be due to the fear that marriages are less likely to result when the dating partners are of such disparate ages. This fear would, of course, be attenuated in a society in which non-marriage was free of stigma.

21. The increase in life expectancy has a much broader impact on contemporary marriage. To make a promise "till death do us part" was, until fairly recently, a rather short-term commitment. Currently, however, it represents a pledge of such long duration that only the most foolhardy would dare to undertake to fulfill it, except under duress.

22. Preferably, a sizable proportion of the caretakers would be males. This departure from standard practice would provide the children with a more natural balance of the sexes among the adults in their environment than is usual in most institutions or in most family settings (the father being away for most of the child's waking hours). The change can come about if salaries are high enough and if women are successful in liberating themselves from the stereotype of being peculiarly well suited for child-care.

23. For interesting alternatives in educational methods, see Neill. 1960; and Skinner, 1962.

24. "The American family no longer is the dominant socializing agency it once was. This loss to the family is a decided gain for the society in the sense that the newer arrangement for socialization more nearly produces the kind of individual we want in view of the kind of society in which we anticipate he will have to live" (Kenkel, 1960, p. 254).

25. Indeed, it quite explicitly attempts to provide for what Parsons (in Parsons & Bales, 1955, pp. 16–17) has called "the basic and irreducible functions" of the American family—the stabilization of adult personality and the socialization of children—as well as the other traditional functions described in Chapters I and II.

26. See, for example, Calverton (1928).

27. "Feelings of insecurity!...The marriage system trades on them!" (Skinner, 1962, p. 146). It would be a gross overstatement, of course, to assert that all persons who choose to marry are emotionally disturbed, or that those who opt for non-marriage are necessarily models of mental health.

Bibliography

NOTE: Numbers in brackets after bibliographic entries refer to the original source pages from which direct quotes were taken.

Adams, J. T. *Provincial society*. New York: Macmillan, 1927. [pp. 10–11]

Adams, S. H. A sabbatical year for marriage. *Harper's*, 1927–1928, **156**, 94–100. [p. 94]

Alpert, A. Introductory remarks. *Journal of the American Academy of Child Psychiatry*, 1965, **4**, 163–167. [p. 165]

Anderson, J. E. Personality organization in children. *American Psychologist*, 1948, **3**, 409–416. [p. 410]

Angermeirer, W. F., Phelps, J. B., & Reynolds, H. H. The effects of differential early rearing upon discrimination learning in monkeys. *Psychonomic Science*, 1967, **8**, 379–380.

Askew, M. W. Courtly love: Neurosis as an institution. *Psychoanalytic Review*, 1965, **52**, 19–29.

Augustine, Saint. On the good of marriage [De bono conjugali]. In P. Schaff (Ed.), *A select library of Nicene and post-Nicene fathers of the Christian church*. Grand Rapids, Michigan: Wm. B. Eerdmans, 1956.

Babcock, C. G. Some psychodynamic factors in foster parenthood. Part I. *Child Welfare*, 1965, **44**, 485–490.

Baber, R. E. Marriage and the family. (2nd ed.) New York: McGraw-Hill, 1953. [pp. 569,27,34,539]

Baker, R. A remarkable experiment. *American Magazine*, 1907, **63** (1), 227–240.

Bakwin, H. Emotional deprivation in infants. *Journal of Pediatrics*, 1949, **35**, 512–521. [p. 519]

———. Feeding program for infants. *Federation Proceedings*, 1964, **23**, 66–68,

Bakwin, H., & Bakwin, R. M. *Clinical management of beheavior disorders in children*. (2nd ed.) Philadelphia: Saunders, 1960. [p. 412]

Balint, M. On genital love. *International Journal of Psycho-analysis*, 1948, **29**, 34–40. [p. 38]

211

Banham, K. M. The development of affectionate behavior in infancy. *Journal of Genetic Psychology*, 1950, **76**, 283–289.

Barnes, A. C. (Ed.) *The social responsibility of gynecology and obstetrics*. Baltimore: Johns Hopkins Press, 1965. [pp. 98,98]

Bartlett, G. A. *Men, women and conflict*. New York: Putnam, 1931. [p.159]

Baumrind, D. Current patterns of parental authority. *Developmental Psychology Monographs*, 1971, **4** (No. 1, Part 2), 1–103.

Beck, E. C., Dustman, R. E., & Sakai, M. Electrophysiological correlates of selective attention. In C. R. Evans & T. B. Mulholland (Eds.), *Attention in neurophysiology*. London: Butterworths, 1969.

Becker, H., & Hill, R. *Marriage and the family*. Boston: Heath, 1942. [p.629]

———. *Family, marriage and parenthood*, Boston: Heath, 1948. [p. 782]

Beckett, P. G., Frohman, C. E., Gottlieb, J. S., Mowbray, J., & Wolf, R. C. Schizophrenic-like mechanisms in monkeys. *American Journal of Psychiatry*, 1963, **119**, 835–842.

Bell, R. R. Some factors related to coed marital aspirations. *Family Life Coordinator*, 1962, **11**, 91–94.

Bender, L. The brain and child behavior. *Archives of General Psychiatry*, 1961, **4**, 531–547.

Berger, P. L., & Kellner, H. Die Ehe und die Konstruktion der Wirklichkeit— Eine Abhandlung zur Mikrosoziologie des Wissens. *Soziale Welt*, 1965, **16**, 220–235. (English translation: Marriage and the construction of reality. *Diogenes*, 1964, **46**, 1–24) [p. 22]

Bergler, E. *Counterfeit-sex: Homosexuality, impotence, frigidity*. (2nd ed.) New York: Grove, 1958.

Bergler, E., & Roheim, G. Psychology of time perception. *Psychanalytic Quarterly*, 1946, **15**, 190–206.

Berkson, J. Mortality and marital status: Reflections on the derivation of etiology from statistics. *American Journal of Public Health*, 1962, **52**, 1318–1329.

Bernard, J. The paradox of the happy marriage. In V. Gornick & B. Moran (Eds.), *Woman in sexist society: Studies in power and powerlessness*. New York: Basic Books, 1971. [p. 94]

Bertoye, P. Le comportement psychique des nourrissons placés en pouponnière. *Annales de Pédiatrie*, 1957, **33**, 353–358.

Beskow, B. Mental disturbances in premature children at school age. *Acta Paediatrica*, 1949, **37**, 125–147.

Bexton, W. H., Heron, W., & Scott, T. H. Effects of decreased variation in the sensory environment. *Canadian Journal of Psychology*, 1954, **8**, 70–76. [p. 70]

Beyle, M. H. [Stendhal]. *On love*. Translated by V. B. Holland. New York; Liveright, 1947 (orig. pub., 1822).

Bierce, A. *The devil's dictionary*, New York: Dover, 1958, (orig. pub., 1911).

Bindra, D. Presentation, In J. M. Tanner & B. Inhelder (Eds.), *Discussions on child development* Vol. 2, New York; International Universities Press, 1954. [pp. 228, 89]

Birdwhistell, R. L. The American family: Some perspectives. *Psychiatry*, 1966, **29**, 203–212.

Blake, J. Population policy for Americans: Is the government being misled? *Science*, 1969, **164**, 522–529. [p. 529]

Blood, R. O. Resolving family conflicts. *Journal of Conflict Resolution*, 1960, **4**, 209–219.

Bodman, F. Constitutional factors in institution children. *Journal of Mental Science*, 1950, **96**, 245–253.

Boffey, P. M. Japan: A crowded nation wants to boost its birthrate. *Science*, 1970, **167**, 960–962.

Booth, M. *Woman and society*. London: George Allen & Unwin, 1929.

Bossard, J., & Boll, E. S. *Why marriages go wrong*. New York: Ronald Press, 1958.

Bovard, E. W., Jr. A theory to account for the effects of early handling on viability of the albino rat. *Science*, 1954, **120**, 187.

Bowlby, J. *Maternal care and mental health*. Geneva: World Health Organization, 1951.

———. Grief and mourning in infancy and early childhood. *Psychoanalytic Study of the Child*, 1960, **15**, 9–52.

Bowlby, J., Ainsworth, M., Boston, M., & Rosenbluth, D. The effects of mother-child separation: A follow-up study. *British Journal of Medical Psychology*, 1956, **29**, 211–247.

Brackbill, Y. Extinction of the smiling response in infants as a function of reinforcement schedule. *Child Development*, 1958, **29**, 115–124.

Brennemann, J. The infant ward. *American Journal of Diseases of Children*, 1932, **43**, 577–584.

Bressler, B., Silverman, A. J., Cohen, S. I., & Shmavonian, B. Research in human subjects and the artificial traumatic neurosis: Where does our responsibility lie? *American Journal of Psychiatry*, 1959, **116**, 522–526.

Briffault, R. *The mothers*. New York: Macmillan, 1927. 3 vols. [Vol. II, pp. 1, 165, Vol. III, p. 244, Vol. I, pp. 508, 522, 286, Vol. III, p. 368, Vol. II, p. 28, Vol. I., pp. 602–603]

———. Taboos on human nature. In V. F. Calverton & S. D. Schmalhausen (Eds.), *The new generation*. New York: Macaulay, 1930. [pp. 434, 685]

———. Free love. *Encyclopedia of the Social Sciences*, 1931, **6**, 433–436.

Briffault, R., & Malinowski, B. *Marriage: Past and present*. Boston: Porter Sargent, 1956. [pp. 50, 90, 57]

Broderick, C. B. Dating and mating among teenagers. *Medical Aspects of Human Sexuality*, 1968, **2** (8), 16–19. [p. 18]

Brody, S. *Patterns of mothering*. New York: International Universities Press, 1956. [p. 100]

Broom, L., & Selznick, P. *Sociology*. (2nd ed.) Evanston: Row, Peterson, 1958. [p. 84]

Brown, S. May I ask you a few questions about love? *Saturday Evening Post*, 31 December 1966, pp. 24–27.

Bühler, K. *The mental development of the child*. Translated by O. Oeser. New York: Harcourt-Brace, 1930 (orig. pub., 1919).

Burgess, E. W., & Wallin, P. *Engagement and marriage*. Philadelphia: Lippincott, 1953.

Cadwallader, M. Marriage as a wretched institution. *Atlantic*, 1966, **218** (November), 62–66.

———. In search of adulthood. In S. M. Farber & R. H. Wilson (Eds.), *Teenage marriage and divorce*. Berkeley: Diablo Press, 1967. [pp. 18, 19–20]

Cairns, R. B. Attachment behavior of mammals. *Psychological Review*, 1966, **73**, 409–426. [pp. 420–421]

Caldwell, B. M. What is the optimal learning environment for the young child? *American Journal of Orthopsychiatry*, 1967, **37**, 8–21.

Calverton, V. F. *The bankruptcy of marriage*. New York: Macaulay, 1928. [p. 232]

Calverton, V. F., & Schmalhausen, S. D. *The new generation*. New York: Macaulay, 1930. [p. 189]

Cantarow, E., Diggs, E., Ellis, K., Marx, J., Robinson, L., & Schein, M. On women's liberation. In H. Gadlin & B. Gerskof (Eds.), *The uptight society: A book of readings*. Belmont, Cal.: Brooks/Cole, 1970.

Casler, L. Maternal deprivation: A critical review of the literature. *Monographs of the Society for Research in Child Development*, 1961, **26** (2), 1–64.

———. The effects of extra tactile stimulation on a group of institutionalized infants. *Genetic Psychology Monographs*, 1965, **71**, 137–175.

———. The effects of supplementary verbal stimulation on a group of institutionalized infants. *Journal of Child Psychology and Psychiatry*, 1965, **6**, 19–27.

———. Perceptual deprivation in institutional settings. In G. Newton & S. Levine (Eds.), *Early experience and behavior*. Springfield, Ill.: Charles C Thomas, 1968.

———. This thing called love is pathological. *Psychology Today*, 1969, **3** (12) 18 ff.

———. Marriage motives in two college populations. *Personality*, 1970, **1**, 220–229.

———. Toward a re-evaluation of love. In M. E. Curtin (Ed.), *Symposium on love*. New York: Behavioral Publications, 1973.

———. Supplementary verbal and vestibular stimulation: Effects on institutionalized infants. Unpublished manuscript.

Christensen, H. T. Cultural relativism and premarital sex norms. *American Sociological Review*, 1960, **25**, 31–39. [p. 39]

Christensen, H. T., & Philbrick, R. E. Family size as a factor in the marital adjustments of college couples. *American Sociological Review*, 1952, **18**, 306–312.

Christenson, C. V., & Gagnon, J. H. Sexual behavior in a group of older women. *Journal of Gerontology*, 1965, **20**, 351–356.

Christie, R. Experimental naïveté and experiential naïveté. *Psychological Bulletin*, 1951, **48**, 327–339.

Church, C. C. Communism in marriage. *Nation*, 1926, **123**, 124–126. [p. 125]

Clarkson, F. E., Vogel, S. R., Broverman, I. K., Broverman, D. M., & Rosenkrantz, P. S. Family size and sex-role stereotype. *Science*, 1970, **167**, 390–392.

Codrington, R. H. *The Melanesians: Their anthropology and folklore*. London: Oxford Press, 1891.

Cohen, C. *Sex and religion*. London: Foulis, 1919.

Coppinger, R. M., & Rosenblatt, P. C. Romantic love and subsistence dependence of spouses. *Southwestern Journal of Anthropology*, 1968, **24**, 310–319. [p. 318]

Crandall, V. J., Dewey, R., Katkovsky, W., & Preston, A. Parents' attitudes and behaviors and grade-school children's academic achievements. *Journal of Genetic Psychology*, 1964, **104**, 53–66.

Dai, B. Personality problems in Chinese culture. *American Siological Review*, 1941, **6**, 688–696.

Davenport, R. K., & Menzel, E. W. Stereotyped behavior of the infant chimpanzee. *Archives of General Psychiatry*, 1963, **8**, 99–104. [p. 104]

Davis, K. *Human society*. New York: Macmillan, 1954.

de Beauvoir, S. *The second sex*. Translated by H. M. Parshley. New York: Bantam Books, 1961 (orig. French ed., 1949). [pp. 418, 419, 127, 406, 655, 452]

de LaPouge, G. V. Die Crisis der Sexuellen Moral. *Politisch-anthropologische Revue*, 1908, **7**, 408–423.

de Lissovoy, V. Head banging in early childhood: A suggested cause. *Journal of Genetic Psychology*, 1963, **102**, 109–114.

deLys, C. *A treasury of parenthood and its folklore*. New York: Speller & Sons, 1958. [p. 33]

Demosthenes. Against Neaera. In *Collected works*, vol. 6. Translated by A. T. Murray. Cambridge: Harvard University Press, 1964. [pp. 445–447]

Dennis, W. Causes of retardation among institutional children: Iran. *Journal of Genetic Psychology*, 1960, **96**, 47–59. [p. 59]

Dennis, W., & Najarian, P. Infant development under environmental handicap. *Psychological Monographs*, 1957, **71** (7), 1–13. [p. 7]

De Pomerai, R. *Marriage, past, present and future*. London: Constable, 1930. [pp. 307, 311, 305]

de Rougemont, D. *Love in the western world*. (Rev. ed.) New York: Pantheon, 1956. [p. 300]

Despert, J. L. Anxiety, phobias, fears in young children, with special reference to prenatal, natal, and neonatal factors. *Nervous Child*, 1946, **5**, 8–24.

de Tocqueville, A. *Democracy in America*. Translated by H. Reeve. (Rev. ed.) New York: Knopf, 1945. 2 vols. (orig. pub., 1840) [Vol. 2, pp. 201, 202, 212]

Deutsch, H. An introduction to the discussion of the psychological problems of pregnancy. In M. J. Senn (Ed.), *Problems of early infancy. Transactions of the second conference (1948)*. New York: Josiah Macy, Jr. Foundation, 1951. (orig. pub., 1949)

Devereux, G. *A study of abortion in primitive societies*. New York: Julian Press, 1954. [p. 161]

DiBartolo, R., & Vinacke, W. E. Relationship between adult nurturance and dependency and performance of the preschool child. *Developmental Psychology*, 1969, **1**, 247–251.

Drever, J. Early learning and the perception of space. *American Journal of Psychology*, 1955, **68**, 605–614.

Dublin, L. I. *Suicide: A sociological and statistical study*. New York: Ronald Press, 1963.

Dührssen, A. *Heimkinder und Pflegekinder in ihrer Entwicklung*. Göttingen: Verlag für Medizinische Psychologie, 1958.

Durfee, H., & Wolf, K. Anstaltspflege und Entwicklung im 1. Lebensjahr. *Zeitschrift für Kinderforschung*, 1933, **42**, 273–320.

Dyer, D. T., & Luckey, E. B. Religious affiliation and selected personality scores as they relate to marital happiness of a Minnesota college sample. *Marriage and Family Living*, 1961, **23**, 46–47.

Dykstra, J. W. Pro-natal influences in American culture. *Sociology and Social Research*, 1959, **44**, 79–85. [p. 84]

Eaton, J. W., & Weil, R. J. *Culture and mental disorders*. Glencoe, Ill.: Free Press, 1955.

Eckland, B. K. Theories of mate selection. *Eugenics Quarterly*, 1968, **15**, 71–84.

Edwards, J. N. The future of the family revisited. *Journal of Marriage and the Family*, 1967, **29**, 505–511.

Eisen, N. H. Some effects of early sensory deprivation on later behavior: The quondam hard-of-hearing child. *Journal of Abnormal and Social Psychology*, 1962, **65**, 338–342.

Ellis, A. Some significant correlates of love and family attitudes and behavior. *Journal of Social Psychology*, 1949, **30**, 3–16.

————. *The American sexual tragedy*, New York: Grove, 1962.

————. Group marriage: A possible alternative. In H. Otto (Ed.), *The family in search of a future*. New York: Appleton-Century-Crofts, 1970. [p. 92]

Ellis, H. Sex in relation to society. *Studies in the psychology of sex*, vol. 6. Philadelphia: Davis, 1910. [pp. 488, 417, 450, 421, 473, 472]

Engels, F. *The origin of the family, private property, and the state*. Translated by E. Untermann. Chicago: Charles Kerr, 1902. (orig. pub., 1884)

English, O. S., & Pearson, G. H. *Emotional problems of living*. (Rev. ed.) New York: Norton, 1955. [p. 55]

Eriksen, C. W. Personality. *Annual Review of Psychology*, 1957, **8**, 185–210. [pp. 194–195]

Espinas, A. *Des sociétés animales*, Paris: Librairie Germer Baillière, 1878.

Fawcett, J. T. Psychology and childbearing. Washington, D. C.: Population Reference Bureau, PRB Selection No. 39, 1971 (Sept.), 1–5.

Feldman, H. Development of the husband-wife relationship. Mimeographed: Ithaca: Cornell University, 1964.

Fischer, L. K. The significance of a typical postural and grasping behavior during the first year of life. *American Journal of Orthopsychiatry*, 1958, **28**, 368–375. [p. 371]

Flügel, J. C. *The psycho-analytic study of the family*. London: Hogarth, 1926. [p. 159]

Foote, N. N. Family, *Encyclopædia Britannica*, 1960, **9**, 59–63. [p. 60]

Fortune, R. F. *Sorcerers of Dobu*. New York: Dutton, 1932.

Francis de Sales, Saint. *Introduction to the devout life*. Edited by J. K. Ryan. New York: Harper & Row, 1966. (orig. pub., 1609) [p. 186]

Frank, L. K. The psychocultural approach in sex research. *Social Problems*, 1954, **1**. 3–136.

―――. Tactile communication. *Genetic Psychology Monographs*, 1957, **56**, 209–255. [p. 220]

French, J. D. The reticular formation. In J. Field (Ed.), *Handbook of physiology. Section 1: Neurophysiology*. Vol. 2. Washington, D. C.: American Physiological Society, 1960.

Freud, A. Discussion of Dr. John Bowlby's paper. *Psychoanalytic Study of the Child*, 1960, **15**, 53–62. [p. 59]

Freud, A., & Burlingham, D. *Infants without families*. New York: International Universities Press, 1944. [p. 12]

Freud, A., & Dann, S. An experiment in group upbringing. *Psychoanalytic Study of the Child*, 1951, **6**, 127–168. [pp. 167–168]

Freud, S. *Group psychology and the analysis of the ego*. Translated by J. Strachey. London: International Psycho-analytic Press, 1922. (orig. pub., 1921)

Friedan, B. *The feminine mystique*. New York: Norton, 1963.

Friedland, R. If we understood Bergman, we'd stone him. *New York Times*, 27 May 1973, p. D-11.

Friedman, C., Handford, A., & Settlage, E. Child psychologic development: the adverse effects of physical restraint. Paper presented at the regional meeting of the American Psychiatric Association, Philadelphia, April, 1964.

Gass, G. Z. Counseling implications of woman's changing role. *Personnel and Guidance Journal*, 1959, **37**, 482–487.

Geber, M. The psychomotor development of African children in the first year, and the influence of maternal behavior. *Journal of Social Psychology*, 1958a, **47**, 185–195. [p. 194]

―――. Testes de Gesell et de Terman-Merrill appliqués en Uganda. *Enfance*, 1958b, No. 1, 63–67.

―――. Longitudinal study and psycho-motor development among Baganda children. In G. Nielson (Ed.), *Proceedings of the XIV International Congress of Applied Psychology*. Vol. 3. *Child and education*. Copenhagen: Munksgaard, 1962.

Gebhard, P. H., Pomeroy, W. B., Martin, C. E., & Christensen, C. V. *Pregnancy, birth and abortion*. New York: Harper, 1958.

Gelinier-Ortigues, M., & Aubry, J. Maternal deprivation, psychogenic deafness and pseudo-retardation. In G. Caplan (Ed.), *Emotional problems of early childhood*. New York: Basic Books, 1955.

Gerson, A. Die Ursachen der Prostitution. B. Psychologische Ursachen. *Sexuale-Probleme*, 1908, **4**, 538–570. Cited by H. Ellis, *Studies in the psychology of sex*, Vol. 6. Philadelphia: Davis, 1910. [p. 495]

Gesell, A. Behavior aspects of the care of the premature infant. *Journal of Pediatrics*, 1946, **29**, 210–212.

Gewirtz, J. L. A learning analysis of the effects of normal stimulation, privation, and deprivation on the acquisition of social motivation and attachment. In B. M. Foss (Ed.), *Determinants of infant behavior*. Vol. 1. New York: Wiley, 1961.

―――. On defining the functional environment of the child: The facilitation of behavioral development by differential stimulation. Mimeographed: New York: Early Child Care Reexamined Committee, February 1966.

———. On designing the functional environment of the child to facilitate behavioral development. In L. L. Dittmann (Ed.), *New perspectives in early child care*. New York: Atherton, 1968. [p. 200]

Gilliard, E. T. The evolution of bowerbirds. *Scientific American*, 1963, **204** (2), 38–46.

Glaser, K. Implications from maternal deprivation research for practice and theory in child welfare. In H. Witmer (Ed.), *Maternal deprivation*. New York: Child Welfare League, 1962.

Glaser, K., & Eisenberg, L. Maternal deprivation. *Pediatrics*, 1956, **18**, 626–642. [p. 639]

Godfrey, J. A. *The science of sex*. London: University Press, 1901. [p. 123]

Goethe, J. W. *Elective affinities*. Translated by E. Mayer & L. Bogan. Chicago: H. Regnery, 1963 (orig. pub., 1808).

Goldfarb, W. Emotional and intellectual consequences of psychological deprivation in infancy: A revaluation. In P. H. Hoch & J. Zubin (Eds.), *Psychopathology of childhood*. New York: Grune & Stratton, 1955.

Goldhamer, H., & Marshall, A. W. *Psychosis and civilization*. Glencoe, Ill.: Free Press, 1953.

Goldstein, K. *The organism*. New York: American, 1939 (orig. pub., 1934). [Chap. 7]

Goode, W. J. The theoretical importance of love. *American Sociological Review*, 1959, **24**, 38–47. [p. 38]

———. Illegitimacy in the Caribbean social structure. *American Sociological Review*, 1960, **25**, 21–30.

———. Family disorganization. In R. K. Merton & R. A. Nisbet (Eds.), *Contemporary social problems*. New York: Harcourt, Brace, & World, 1961. [pp. 441–442]

———. Marital satisfaction and instability: A cross-cultural class analysis of divorce rates. *International Social Science Journal*, 1962, **14**, 507–527. [p. 513]

———. *The family*. Englewood Cliffs, N. J.: Prentice-Hall, 1964.

———. Family patterns and human rights. *International Social Science Journal*, 1966, **23**, 41–54. [p. 48]

Gough, E. K. The Nayars and the definition of marriage. *Journal of the Royal Anthropological Institute*, 1959, **89**, 23–34.

Gray, H. Marriage and premarital conception. *Journal of Psychology*, 1960, **50**, 383–397.

Green, P. C., & Gordon, M. Maternal deprivation: Its influence on visual exploration in infant monkeys. *Science*, 1964, **145**, 292–294.

Greenfield, S. M. Love and marriage in modern America: A functional analysis. *Sociological Quarterly*, 1965, **6**, 361–377. [p. 374]

———. The Bruce effect and Malinowski's hypothesis on mating and fertility. *American Anthropologist*, 1968, **70**, 759–760.

Greenwald, H. Marriage as a non-legal voluntary association. In H. Otto (Ed.), *The family in search of a future*. New York: Appleton-Century-Crofts, 1970.

Greenwood, D. *Essays in human relations*. Washington, D. C.: Public Affairs Press, 1956.

Groves, E. R. *Marriage*. (Rev. ed.) New York: Henry Holt, 1941. [pp. 613, 607, 1, 550]

Guttmacher, M. S., & Weihofen, H. *Psychiatry and the law*. New York: Norton, 1952. [p. 91]

György, P., Dhanamitta, S., & Steers, E. Protective effects of human milk in experimental staphylococcus infection. *Science*, 1962, **137**, 338–340.

Hadden, J. K., & Borgatta, M. L. (Eds.) *Marriage and the family*. Itasca, Ill.: F. E. Peacock, 1969.

Haire, N. *Hymen; or the future of marriage*. London: Routledge & Kegan Paul, 1927. [pp. 8, 67]

Hamilton, G. V. *A research in marriage*. New York: Albert & Charles Boni, 1929.

Harlow, H. F. The nature of love. *American Psychologist*, 1958, **13**, 673–685.

———. The development of affectional patterns in infant monkeys. In B. M. Foss (Ed.), *Determinants of infant behavior*. Vol. 1. New York: Wiley, 1961.

Harlow, H. F., & Harlow, M. K. The effect of rearing conditions on behavior. *Bulletin of the Menninger Clinic*, 1962a, **26**, 213–224.

———. Social deprivation in monkeys. *Scientific American*, 1962b, **207** (5), 136–146. [p. 138].

———. Learning to love. *American Scientist*, 1966, **54**, 244–272.

Hart, H., & Hart, E. B. *Personality and the family*. (Rev. ed.) Boston: Heath, 1941.

Hatch, A., Balazs, T., Wiberg, G. S., & Grice, H. C. Long-term isolation stress in rats. *Science*, 1963, **142**, 507.

Havighurst, R. J. Cultural factors in sex expression. In A. Deutsch (Ed.), *Sex habits of American men*. New York: Prentice-Hall, 1948.

Hebb, D. O. The mammal and his environment. *American Journal of Psychiatry*, 1955, **101**, 826–831. [p. 827[]

Hefner, H. M. The legal enforcement of morality. *University of Colorado Law Review*, 1968, **40**, 199–221. [pp. 220–221]

Heinlein, R. *Stranger in a strange land*. New York: Putnam, 1961. [p. 345]

Hempel, C. The logic of functional analysis. In L. Gross (Ed.), *Symposium on sociological theory*. Evanston: Row, Peterson, 1959.

Heston, L. L., Denny, D. D., & Pauly I. B. The adult adjustment of persons institutionalized as children. *British Journal of Psychiatry*, 1966, **112**, 1103–1110.

Hicks, M. W., & Platt, M. Marital happiness and stability: A review of the research in the 60's. *Journal of Marriage and the Family*, 1970, **32**, 553–574.

Himelhoch, J., & Fava, S. F. (Eds.) *Sexual behavior in American society*. New York: Norton, 1955.

Hippolytus. *Philosophomena, or the refutation of all heresies*. (Rev. ed.) New York: Ktav, 1972.

Hitler, A. *Mein Kampf*. Translated by J. Chamberlain *et al*. New York: Reynal & Hitchcock, 1939 (orig. pub., 1925).

Hobart, C. W. Commitment, value conflict and the future of the American family. *Marriage and Family Living*, 1963, **25**, 405–412. [p. 409]

Hofer, M. Physiological responses of infant rats to separation from their mothers. *Science*, 1970, **168**, 871–873.

Hoffman, L. W., & Wyatt, F. Social change and motivations for having larger families: Some theoretical considerations. *Merrill-Palmer Quarterly*, 1961, **6**, 235–244.

Holloway, M. *Heavens on earth*. London: Turnstile Press, 1951.

House, S. D. Is consciousness curative? *Psychoanalytic Review*, 1929, **16**, 28–45.

Howe, E. G. Motives and mechanisms of the mind. VII. Love: The role of the mother. *Lancet*, 1931, **220**, 365–370.

Hunt, H. F., & Otis, L. S. Early "experience" and its effects on later behavioral processes in rats: I. Initial experiments. *Transactions of the New York Academy of Sciences*, 1963, **25** (8), 858–870.

Hunt, J. McV. Experience and the development of motivation: Some reinterpretations. *Child Development*, 1960, **31**, 489–504.

Hunt, M. M. *The natural history of love*. New York: Knopf, 1959. [pp. 127, 393]

Hurlock, E. B. *Child development*. (4th ed.) New York: McGraw-Hill, 1964. [p. 69]

Hutchinson, W. Evolutionary ethics of marriage and divorce. *Contemporary Review*, 1905, **88**, 397–410.

Illingworth, R. S. Crying in infants and children. *British Medical Journal*, 1955, No. 1, pp. 75–78.

Irvine, E. E. Observations on the aims and methods of child rearing in communal settlements in Israel. *Human Relations*, 1952, **5**, 247–275.

———. Children in kibbutzim: thirteen years after. *Journal of Child Psychology and Psychiatry*, 1966, **7**, 167–178.

Jackson, C. W., Jr., & Pollard, J. C. Sensory deprivation and suggestion: A theoretical approach. *Behavioral Science*, 1962, **7**, 332–342.

Jacobs, B. Aetiological factors and reaction types in psychoses following childbirth. *Journal of Mental Science*, 1943, **89**, 242–256.

Jaffe, F. S., & Guttmacher, A. F. Family planning programs in the United States. *Demography*, 1968, **5**, 910–923.

Jenkins, S. Filial deprivation in parents of children in foster care. *Children*, 1967, **14**, 8–12.

Jersild, A. T. *Child psychology*. (6th ed.) Englewood Cliffs, N. J.: Prentice-Hall, 1968.

Journal of the American Medical Association. Editorial: The battered child syndrome. 1962, **181**, 42.

Jourard, S. Reinventing marriage: The perspective of a psychologist. In H. Otto (Ed.), *The family in search of a future*. New York: Appleton-Century-Crofts, 1970.

Kaufman, I. C., & Rosenblum, L. A. Depression in infant monkeys separated from their mothers. *Science*, 1967, **155**, 1030–1031.

Kelly, E. L. Consistency of the adult personality. *American Psychologist*, 1955, **10**, 659–681.

Kelsen, H. Platonic love. *American Imago*, 1942, **3**, 3–110.

Kenkel, W. F. *The family in perspective*. New York: Appleton-Century-Crofts, 1960. [pp. 42, 15–16, 120, 78, 324]

Key, E. *The century of the child*. New York: Putnam, 1909.

Kinsey, A. C., Pomeroy, W. B., & Martin, C. E. *Sexual behavior in the human male*. Philadelphia: Saunders, 1948. [p. 589]

Kinsey, A. C., Pomeroy, W. B., Martin, C. E., & Gebhard, P. H. *Sexual behavior in the human female*. Philadelphia: Saunders, 1953. [p. 20, 482]

Kistyakovskaya, M. Y. O stimulakh vyzyvayushchikh polozhitel'nye emotsii v rebenka pervykh mesyatsev zhizni. *Voprosy Psikhologii*, 1965, **2**, 129–140. (*Psychological Abstracts*, 1965, **39**, 1322)

Klackenberg, G. Studies in maternal deprivation in infants' homes. *Acta Paediatrica*, 1956, **45**, 1–12. [p. 7]

Klineberg, O. *Social psychology*. (Rev. ed.) New York: Henry Holt, 1954.

Kluijver, H. N. The population ecology of the great tit, *Parus m. major L. Ardea*, 1951, **39**, 1–135.

Koestler, A. Man—one of evolution's mistakes? *New York Times Magazine*, 19 October 1969, p. 28, ff. [p. 112]

Korner, A. F., & Thoman, E. B. Visual alertness in neonates as evoked by maternal care. *Journal of Experimental Child Psychology*, 1970, **10**, 67–78.

Kubie, L. S. Psychiatric implications of the Kinsey report. *Psychosomatic Medicine*, 1948, **10**, 95–106. [p. 105]

————. Psychoanalysis and marriage. In V. W. Eisenstein (Ed.), *Neurotic interaction in marriage*. New York: Basic Books, 1956. [p. 30]

Kuhlen, R. G. Aging and life adjustment. In J. E. Birren (Ed.), *Handbook of aging and the individual*. Chicago: University of Chicago Press, 1959.

Kunst, M. S. A study of thumb- and finger-sucking in infants. *Psychological Monographs*, 1948, **62**, No. 3. [p. 68]

La Barre, W. *The human animal*. Chicago: University of Chicago Press, 1954. [p. 63]

Lafitau, J. B. *Moeurs des sauvages amériquains comparées aux moeurs des premiers temps*. Paris: Saugrain l'aîné [etc.], 1724. [Vol. I, p. 536]

Landis, J. T., Poffenberger, T., & Poffenberger, S. The effects of first pregnancy upon the sexual adjustment of 212 couples. *American Sociological Review*, 1950, **15**, 766–772.

Langworthy, O. R. Development of behavioral patterns and myelinization of the nervous system in the human fetus and infant. *Carnegie Institution of Washington: Contributions to Embryology*, 1933, **24**, No. 139.

Launay, C., Verliac, F., Trelat, E., & Lyard, D. Sur l'hôspitalisme et la "carence de soins maternels" dans la petite enfance. *Gazette Médicale de France*, 1956, 63–64, 291–301.

Lehrman, D. S. The physiological basis of parental feeding behavior in the ring dove (*Streptopelia risoria*). *Behaviour*, 1955, **7**, 241–286.

————. Psi Chi address (unpublished), Geneseo, New York, 1972.

Leiderman, H., Mendelson, J. H., Wexler, D., & Solomon, P. Sensory deprivation. *AMA Archives of Internal Medicine*, 1958, **101**, 389–396. [p. 394]

LeMasters, E. E. Parenthood as a crisis. *Marriage and Family Living*, 1957, **19**, 352–355.

Lemmon, W. B., & Patterson, G. H. Depth perception in sheep: Effects of interrupting the mother-neonate bond. *Science*, 1964, **145**, 835–836.

Leslie, G. R. *The family in social context*. New York: Oxford University Press, 1967.

Lessac, M. S., & Solomon, R. L. Effects of early isolation on the later adaptive behavior of beagles: A methodological demonstration. *Developmental Psychology*, 1969, **1**, 14–25.

Levi, W. *The pigeon*. Sumpter [sic], S. C.: Levi Publishing Company, 1957.

Levinger, G. Marital cohesiveness and dissolution: An integrative review. *Journal of Marriage and the Family*, 1965, **27**, 19–28.

Levinson, B. M. Parental achievement drives for preschool children, the Vineland Social Maturity Scale, and the social deviation quotient. *Journal of Genetic Psychology*, 1961, **99**, 113–128.

Levy, D. M. On the problem of movement restraint. *American Journal of Orthopsychiatry*, 1944, **14**, 644–671. [p. 655]

Levy, M. J., Jr., & Fallers, L. A. The family: some comparative considerations. *American Anthropologist*, 1959, **61**, 647–651.

Lewinsohn, R. *A history of sexual customs*. Translated by A. Mayce. New York: Harper, 1958. (orig. pub. 1956) [p. 222]

Liddell, H. S. Sheep and goats: The psychological effects of laboratory experiences of deprivation upon certain experimental animals. In I. Galdston (Ed.), *Beyond the germ theory*. New York: Health Education Council, 1954.

Lilly, J. C. Mental effects of reduction of ordinary levels of physical stimuli on intact, healthy persons. *Psychiatric Research Reports*, 1956, **5**, 1–9. [p. 4]

Lindsey, B. B., & Evans, W. *The companionate marriage*. New York: Boni & Liveright, 1927.

Lindzey, G. Some remarks concerning incest, the incest taboo, and psychoanalytic theory. *American Psychologist*, 1967, **22**, 1051–1059.

Linton, R. *The study of man*. New York: Appleton-Century-Crofts, 1936. [p. 175]

Livingstone, W. P. *Black Jamaica: A study in evolution*. London: Sampson Low, 1899. [pp. 213–214]

Locke, H. J. *Predicting adjustment in marriage*. New York: Holt, Rinehart, & Winston, 1951.

Lowie, R. H. *Primitive society*. New York: Boni & Liveright, 1920. [p. 66]

——. Marriage. *Encyclopedia of the Social Sciences*, 1933, **10**, 146–154. [p. 150]

Lowrey, L. G. Personality distortion and early institutional care. *American Journal of Orthopsychiatry*, 1940, **10**, 576–585.

Ludlow, W. L. *A syllabus and a bibliography of marriage and the family*. New Concord, Ohio: Radcliffe Press, 1951. [p. 37]

Maas, H. S., & Engler, R. E. *Children in need of parents*. New York: Columbia University Press, 1959.

Malinowski, B. Parenthood—the basis of social structure. In V. F. Calverton & S. D. Schmalhausen (Eds.), *The new generation*. New York: Macaulay, 1930.

——. Marriage. *Encyclopædia Britannica*, 1960, **14**, 940–950. [pp. 940, 950, 943, 942, 945]

Mannes, M. *But will it sell?* Philadelphia: Lippincott, 1964. [p. 61]

Marro, A. Problems in eugenics. Report of the First International Eugenics Congress, London, 1912, pp. 118–136. Cited by M. F. A. Montagu, *Prenatal influences*. Springfield, Ill.: Charles C Thomas, 1962. p. 143.

Martinson, F. M. Ego deficiency as a factor in marriage. *American Sociological Review*, 1955, **20**, 161–164.

Mason, W. A., Davenport, R. K., Jr., & Menzel, E. W., Jr. Early experience and the social development of rhesus monkeys and chimpanzees. In G. Newton & S. Levine (Eds.), *Early experience and behavior*. Springfield, Ill.: Charles C Thomas, 1968.

May, G. *Social control of sex expression*. New York: William Morrow, 1931. [pp. 33, 32, 14–15, 44]

Mayer, J. Toward a non-Malthusian population policy. *Columbia Forum*, 1969, **12** (2), 5–13. [p. 6]

McClelland, W. J. Differential handling and weight gain in the albino rat. *Canadian Journal of Psychology*, 1956, **10**, 19–22.

McIntire, R. Parent training or mandatory birth control: take your choice. *Psychology Today*, 1973, **7** (5), 34, ff.

McKinney, J. P., & Keele, T. Effects of increased mothering on the behavior of severely retarded boys. *American Journal of Mental Deficiency*, 1963, **67**, 556–562.

Mead, M. *Coming of age in Samoa*. In M. Mead, *From the south seas*. New York: William Morrow, 1939. [pp. 212, 214, 209]

————. *Male and female*. New York: William Morrow, 1949. [p. 266]

————. Some theoretical considerations on the problem of mother-child separation. *American Journal of Orthopsychiatry*, 1954, **24**, 471–483.

————. Introduction to *American women: The changing image*, by B. B. Cassara. Boston: Beacon Press, 1962. [p. xii]

Meier, R. L. *Modern science and the human fertility problem*. New York: Wiley, 1959.

Melzack, R., & Scott, T. H. The effects of early experience on the response to pain. *Journal of Comparative and Physiological Psychology*, 1957, **50**, 155–161. [p. 160]

Mendelson, J., Solomon, P., & Lindemann, E. Hallucinations of poliomyelitis patients during treatment in a respirator. *Journal of Nervous and Mental Disease*, 1958, **126**, 421–428.

Merton, R. K. *Social theory and social structure*. (Rev. ed.) Glencoe, Ill.: Free Press, 1957.

Merton, R. K., & Barber, E. Sociological ambivalence. In E. A. Tiryakian (Ed.), *Sociological theory, values, and sociocultural change: Essays in honor of Pitirim A. Sorokin*. New York: Free Press, 1963. [p. 111]

Meyer, J. S., Greifenstein, F., & Devault, M. A new drug causing symptoms of sensory deprivation. *Journal of Nervous and Mental Disease*, 1959, **129**, 54–61.

Miller, N. *The child in primitive society*. New York: Brentano's, 1928. [pp. 61–68, 51, 40]

Millett, K. *Sexual politics*. Garden City, N. Y.: Doubleday, 1970. [pp. 118–119]

Mitchell, G. D., Raymond, E. J., Ruppenthal, G. C., & Harlow, H. F. Long-term effects of total social isolation upon behavior of rhesus monkeys. *Psychological Reports*, 1966, **18**, 567–580.

Moloney, J. C. *Understanding the Japanese mind*. Westport, Conn.: Greenwood Press, 1968.

Moltz, H., Geller, D., & Levin, R. Maternal behavior in the totally mammecto-mized rat. *Journal of Comparative and Physiological Psychology*, 1967, **64**, 225–229.

Montagu, M. F. A. Constitutional and prenatal factors in infant and child health. In M. J. Senn (Ed.), *Symposium on the healthy personality. Supplement II: Problems of infancy and childhood. Transactions of fourth conference, March, 1950*. New York: Josiah Macy, Jr. Foundation, 1950.

————. The sensory influences of the skin. *Texas Reports on Biology and Medicine*, 1953, **11**, 291–301. [p. 299]

Montaigne, M. *Complete works of . . .* Translated by D. M. Frame. Stanford: Stanford University Press, 1967. (orig. pub., 1580–1587) [p. 649]

Moore, B., Jr. *Political power and social theory*. Cambridge: Harvard University Press, 1958.

Morgan, L. H. *Ancient society*. New York: Henry Holt, 1878.

Morison, R. S. Where is biology taking us? *Science*, 1967, **155**, 429–433. [pp. 432, 430]

Moss, H. A. Review of L. Murphy *et al.*, *The widening world of childhood*. *Merrill-Palmer Quarterly*, 1965, **11**, 171–179. [p. 173]

Moss, H. A., Robson, K. S., & Pedersen, F. Determinants of maternal stimula-tion of infants and consequences of treatment for later reactions to strangers. *Developmental Psychology*, 1969, **1**, 239–246.

Moss, J. J. Why do boys marry? In S. M. Farber & R. H. Wilson (Eds.), *Teen-age marriage and divorce*. Berkeley: Diablo Press, 1967.

Murdock, G. P. *Social structure*. New York: Macmillan, 1949. [p. 10]

————. Sexual behavior: What is acceptable? *Journal of Social Hygiene*, 1950, **36**, 1–31.

Myklebust, H. R. Language disorders in children. *Exceptional Children*, 1956, **22**, 163–166.

Naess, S. Mother separation and delinquency: Further evidence. *British Journal of Criminology*, 1962, **2**, 361–374.

Neal, M. V. Vestibular stimulation and developmental behavior of the small premature infant. *Nursing Research Report*, 1968, **3** (1), 1–5.

Neill, A. S. *Summerhill: A radical approach to child rearing*. New York: Hart, 1960.

Nelson, B. Suicide prevention: NIMH wants more attention for "taboo" sub-ject. *Science*, 1968, **161**, 766–767.

Nilsson, A., Kaij, L., & Jacobson, L. Post-partum mental disorder in an unselected sample: The importance of the unplanned pregnancy. *Journal of Psychosomatic Research*, 1967, **10**, 341–347.

Norris, A. S. Prenatal factors in intellectual and emotional development. *Journal of the American Medical Association*, 1960, **172** (5), 413–416.

O'Connor, N. The evidence for the permanently disturbing effects of mother-child separation. *Acta Psychologica*, 1956, **12**, 174–191. [pp. 189, 186]

Olson, E. (and co-authors). The hazards of immobility. *American Journal of Nursing*, 1967, **67** (1), 779–797.

Oltman, J. E., & Friedman, S. Report on parental deprivation in psychiatric disorders. I. In schizophrenia. *Archives of General Psychiatry*, 1965, **12**, 46–56.

O'Neill, N., & O'Neill, G. *Open marriage*. New York: Avon, 1972. [pp. 22, 195]

Orlansky, H. Infant care and personality. *Psychological Bulletin*, 1949, **46**, 1–48. [p. 16]

Örsten, P., & Mattson, A. Hospitalization symptoms in children. *Acta Paediatrica*, 1955, **44**, 79–92.

Ostwald, P. F., & Regan, P. F., III. Psychiatric disorders associated with childbirth. *Journal of Nervous and Mental Disease*, 1957, **125**, 153–165.

Otto, H. A. (Ed.) *The family in search of a future*. New York: Appleton-Century-Crofts, 1970(a).

———. The group family: A new social concept. In H. A. Otto (Ed.), *The family in search of a future*. New York: Appleton-Century-Crofts, 1970(b), 187–189. [p. 187]

———. The new marriage: Marriage as a framework for developing personal potential. In H. A. Otto (Ed.), *The family in search of a future*. New York: Appleton-Century-Crofts, 1970(c), 111–119. [pp. 112–113]

Packard, V. Relating to your partner. *Today's health*, 1972, **50** (6), 3–35.

Palson, C., & Palson R. Swinging in wedlock. In E. Aronson & R. Helmreich (Eds.), *Social Psychology*. New York: Van Nostrand, 1973.

Parsons, T. The incest taboo in relation to social structure and the socialization of the child. *British Journal of Sociology*, 1954, **5**, 101–117.

Parsons, T., & Bales, R. F. *Family, socialization and interaction process*. Glencoe, Ill.: Free Press, 1955. [pp. 22, 154]

Peshkin, M. M. Asthma in children. *American Journal of Diseases of Children*, 1930, **39**, 774–781.

Piaget, J. *The moral judgment of the child*. Translated by M. Gabain. New York: Harcourt, Brace, 1948 (orig. pub., 1932).

Pineo, P. C. Disenchantment in the later years of marriage. *Marriage and Family Living*, 1961, **23**, 3–11.

Pinneau, S. A critique on the articles by Margaret Ribble. *Child Development*, 1950, **21**, 203–228.

———. The infantile disorders of hospitalism and anaclitic depression. *Psychological Bulletin*, 1955, **52**, 429–452.

Plato. *Laws*. Translated by R. G. Bury. Cambridge: Harvard University Press, 1961. 2 vols.

———. *The Statesman*. Translated by H. N. Fowler. Cambridge: Harvard University Press, 1962.

Ploscowe, M. *Sex and the law*. (Rev. Ed.) New York: Ace, 1962.

Rabin, A. I. Personality maturity of kibbutz (Israeli collective settlement) and non-kibbutz children as reflected in Rorschach findings. *Journal of Projective Techniques*, 1957, **21**, 148–153.

Rabkin, L. Y., & Carr, J. E. (Eds.) *Sourcebook in abnormal psychology*. Boston: Houghton Mifflin, 1967.

Racamier, P. Étude clinique des frustrations précoces. *Revue Française de Psychanalyse*, 1953, **17**, 328–350.

Ravich, R. A. A sort of "natural commune." *New York Times Magazine*, 5 November 1972, p. 75.

Rawlinson, H. G. *India, a short cultural history*. New York: Praeger, 1952.

Reardon, H., Wilson, J. L., & Graham, B. Physiological deviations of premature infants. *American Journal of Diseases of Children*, 1951, **81**, 99–138.

Reed, R. *The modern family*. New York: Knopf, 1929. [pp. 114, 28, 153, 155]

Reich, W. *The mass psychology of fascism*. Translated by T. Wolfe. New York: Orgone Institute, 1946 (orig. pub., 1933).

Reiss, I. L. The universality of the family: A conceptual analysis. *Journal of Marriage and the Family*, 1965, **27**, 443–453.

Rheingold, H. L. The modification of social responsiveness in institutional babies. *Monographs of the Society for Research in Child Development*, 1956, **21**, No. 2.

———.The measurement of maternal care. *Child Development*, 1960, **31**, 565–575.

———. The effect of environmental stimulation upon social and exploratory behavior in the human infant. In B. M. Foss (Ed.), *Determinants of infant behavior*. Vol. 1. New York: Wiley, 1961. [p. 154]

Rheingold, H. L., & Bayley, N. The later effects of an experimental modification of mothering. *Child Development*, 1959, **30**, 363–372. [p. 372]

Rheingold, J. C. *The mother, anxiety, and death*. Boston: Little, Brown, 1967.

Ribble, M. *The rights of infants: Early psychological needs and their satisfactions*. New York: Columbia University Press, 1943.

Riesen, A. Sensory deprivation. In E. Stellar & J. M. Sprague (Eds.), *Progress in physiological psychology*. Vol. 1. New York: Academic Press, 1966.

Robertson, J. Some responses of young children to the loss of maternal care. *Nursing Times*, 1953, **49**, 381–386.

———. Mothering as an influence on early development: A study of well-baby clinic records. *Psychoanalytic Study of the Child*, 1962, **17**, 245–264.

Robson, K. S. The role of eye-to-eye contact in maternal-infant attachment. *Journal of Child Psychology and Psychiatry*, 1967, **8**, 13–25.

Rollin, B. Motherhood: Who needs it? *Look*, 22 September 1970, 15, ff. [pp. 17, 16]

Rose, J. A., & Sonis, M. The use of separation as a diagnostic measure in the parent-child emotional crisis. *American Journal of Psychiatry*, 1959, **116**, 409–415. [p. 414]

Rosenzweig, N. Sensory deprivation and schizophrenia: Some clinical and theoretical similarities. *American Journal of Psychiatry*, 1959, **116**, 326–329. [p. 328]

Rossi, A. S. Transition to parenthood. *Journal of Marriage and the Family*, 1968, **30**, 26–39. [p. 34]

Rothman, P. E. A note on hospitalism. *Pediatrics*, 1962, **30**, 995–999. [p. 995]

Rothschild, B. F. Incubator isolation as a possible contributing factor to the high incidence of emotional disturbance among prematurely born persons. *Journal of Genetic Psychology*, 1967, **110**, 287–304.

Russell, B. Introduction to *The new generation*, by V. F. Calverton & S. D. Schmalhausen (Eds.). New York: Macaulay, 1930.

———.*Marriage and morals*. New York: Liveright, 1957 (orig. pub., 1929). [p. 27, 122]

Ryder, N. B. The character of modern fertility. *Annals of American Academy of Political and Social Science*, 1967, **369**, 26–36. [p. 33]

Sackett, G. P. Some persistent effects of different rearing conditions on pre-adult social behavior of monkeys. *Journal of Comparative and Physiological Psychology*, 1967, **64**, 363–365.

Sait, U. B. *New horizons of the family*. New York: Macmillan, 1938.

Samuels, I. Reticular mechanisms and behavior. *Psychological Bulletin*, 1959, **56**, 1–25.

Sarvis, M. A., & Garcia, B. Etiological variables in autism. *Psychiatry*, 1961, **24**, 307–317.

Sayegh, Y., & Dennis, W. The effect of supplementary experiences upon the behavioral development of infants in institutions. *Child Development*, 1965, **36**, 81–90.

Schaffer, H. R. Objective observations of personality development in early infancy. *British Journal of Medical Psychology*, 1958, **31**, 174–183. [pp. 177–178]

———. Some issues for research in the study of attachment behaviour. In B. M. Foss (Ed.), *Determinants of Infant Behaviour*. Vol. 2, New York: Wiley, 1963. [p. 192]

———. Changes in developmental quotient under two conditions of maternal separation. *British Journal of Social and Clinical Psychology*, 1965, **4**, 39–46.

———. Activity level as a constitutional determinant of infantile reaction to deprivation. *Child Development*, 1966, **37**, 595–602. [p. 600]

Schlesinger, R. (Ed.) *The family in the U.S.S.R.* London: Routledge & Kegan Paul, 1949.

Schmalhausen, S. D. *Why we misbehave*. New York: Oarden City, 1928. [p. 40]

———. Family life: A study in pathology. In V. F. Calverton & S. D. Schmalhausen (Eds.), *The new generation*. New York: Macaulay, 1930. [pp. 275, 278, 293]

Schneider, D. M. Abortion and depopulation on a Pacific island. In B. D. Paul (Ed.), *Health, culture and community*. New York: Russell Sage Foundation, 1955. [p. 222]

Schooley, M. Personality resemblances among married couples. *Journal of Abnormal and Social Psychology*, 1936, **31**, 340–347.

Schopler, E. Early infantile autism and receptor processes. *Archives of General Psychiatry*, 1965, **13**, 327–335.

Schram, L. M. The Monguors of the Kansu-Tibetan frontier: Their origin, history, and social organization. *Transactions of the American Philosophical Society*, 1954, **44** (n.s.), part 1, 1–138.

Schulze, L. The aborigines of the upper and middle Finke River: Their habits and customs, with introductory notes on the physical and natural history features of the country. *Transactions and Proceedings of the Royal Society of South Australia*, 1890, **14**, 210–246.

Schwartz, R. A. The role of family planning in the primary prevention of mental illness. *American Journal of Psychiatry*, 1969, **125**, 1711–1718.

Scott, J. P. Genetics and the development of social behavior in mammals. *American Journal of Orthopsychiatry*, 1962, **32**, 878–893. [p. 886]

————. Social behavior, animal. *International Encyclopedia of the Social Sciences*, 1968, **14**, 342–351. [p. 349]

Selye, H. *The physiology and pathology of exposure to stress*. Montreal: Acta Endocrinologica, 1960.

Shaw, G. B. *Getting married: A disquisitory play*. In *The Bodley Head Bernard Shaw, Collected plays with their prefaces*. Vol. 3. London: Max Reinhardt, 1971 (orig. pub., 1911). [p. 467]

Simon, A. J., & Bass, L. G. Towards a validation of infant testing. *American Journal of Orthopsychiatry*, 1956, **26**, 340–350.

Skinner, B. F. *Walden two*. New York: Macmillan, 1962 (orig. pub., 1948).

Smigel, E. O., & Seiden, R. The decline and fall of the double standard. *Annals of the American Academy of Political and Social Science*, 1968, **376**, 6–17.

Smolen, E. M. Some thoughts on schizophrenia in childhood. *Journal of the American Academy of Child Psychiatry*, 1965, **4**, 443–472.

Solkoff, N., Yaffe, S., Weintraub, D., & Blase, B. Effects of handling on the subsequent developments of premature infants. *Developmental Psychology*, 1969, **1**, 765–768.

Solomon, P., Kubzansky, P. E., Leiderman, P. H., Mendelson, J. H., Trumbull, R., & Wexler, D. (Eds.) *Sensory deprivation*. Cambridge: Harvard University Press, 1961. [p. 362]

Solomon, P., Leiderman, P. H., Mendelson, J., & Wexler, D. Sensory deprivation. *American Journal of Psychiatry*, 1957, **114**, 357–363.

Sorokin, P. A. *Social and cultural dynamics*. New York: American, 1937–1941. 4 vols.

Spengler, J. J. Population problem: In search of a solution. *Science*, 1969, **166**, 1234–1238.

Spiro, M. E. Is the family universal? *American Anthropologist*, 1954, **56**, 839–846.

————. *Kibbutz: Venture in utopia*. Cambridge: Harvard University Press, 1955. [p. 117]

————. Is the family universal? (rev.) In N. W. Bell & E. F. Vogel (Eds.), *A modern introduction to the family*. Glencoe, Ill.: Free Press, 1960.

Spitz, R. A. Diacritic and coenesthetic organization. *Psychoanalytic Review*, 1945, **32**, 146–162. [p. 157]

————. Hospitalism: An inquiry into the genesis of psychiatric conditions in early childhood. Part 1. *Psychoanalytic Study of the Child*, 1945, **1**, 53–74.

————. Psychiatric therapy in infancy. *American Journal of Orthopsychiatry*, 1950, **20**, 623–633.

————. Genèse des premières relations objectales. *Revue Française de Psychanalyse*, 1954, **18**, 477–575. [p. 569]

————. Reply to Dr. Pinneau. *Psychological Bulletin*, 1955, **52**, 453–458.

————. *No and yes*. New York: International Universities Press, 1957.

Spitz, R. A., & Wolf, K. M. Environment vs. race—environment as an etiological factor in psychiatric disturbances in infancy. *Archives of Neurology and Psychiatry*, 1947, **57**, 120–125. [p. 124]

Srole, L., Langner, T. S., Michael, S. T., Opler, M. K., & Rennie, T. A. *Mental health in the metropolis: The midtown Manhattan study*. New York: McGraw-Hill, 1962.

Stekel, W. Frigidity in mothers. In V. F. Calverton & S. D. Schmalhausen (Eds.), *The new generation*. New York: Macaulay, 1930.

Stephens, W. N. A cross-cultural study of menstrual taboos. *Genetic Psychology Monographs*, 1961, **64**, 385–416.

———. *The family in cross-cultural perspective*. New York: Holt, Rinehart, & Winston, 1963.

Stevenson, S. S. Paranatal factors affecting adjustment in childhood. *Pediatrics*, 1948, **2**, 154–162.

Stoller, F. H. The intimate network of families as a new structure. In H. A. Otto (Ed.), *The family in search of a future*. New York: Appleton-Century-Crofts, 1970. [p. 149]

Stott, D. H. Physical and mental handicaps following a disturbed pregnancy. *Lancet*, 1957, **272**, 1006–1012.

———. Abnormal mothering as a cause of mental subnormality: II. Case studies and conclusions. *Journal of Child Psychology and Psychiatry*, 1962, **3**, 133–148.

Strauss, A. The influence of parent-images upon marital choice. *American Sociological Review*, 1946, **11**, 554–559.

Strecker, E. A. *Their mothers' sons*. New York: Lippincott, 1946. [p. 23]

Stycos, J. M. The outlook for world population. *Science*, 1964, **146**, 1435–1440.

Sumner, W. G. *Folkways*. Boston: Ginn, 1940. (orig. pub., 1906) [p. 315]

Sumner, W. G., & Keller, A. G. *The science of society*. New Haven: Yale University Press, 1927. 4 vols. [p. 1894]

Takkunen, R. L., Frisk, M., & Holmström, G. Follow-up examination of 110 small prematures at the age of 6–7 years. *Acta Paediatrica Scandinavica, Supplement*, 1965, **159**, 70–71.

Talmon-Garber, Y. The family in collective settlements. *Transactions of the Third World Congress of Sociology*, 1956, **4**, 116–126.

Temerlin, M. K., Trousdale, W. W., LaCrone, H. H., Harrison, C. H., & Rundell, O. H. Effects of increased mothering and skin contact on retarded boys. *American Journal of Mental Deficiency*, 1967, **71**, 890–893. [p. 893]

Terman, L. *Psychological factors in marital happiness*. New York: McGraw-Hill, 1938. [p. 370]

Tezner, O. Zur Frage der Kinderheime. *Annales Paediatrici*, 1956, **186**, 189–209. [pp. 207–208]

Thamm, R. The distribution of interpersonal involvement: A humanistic theory. Unpublished manuscript.

Thomas, W. I. *Primitive behavior*. New York: McGraw-Hill, 1937.

Thompson, W. R. Early environmental influences on behavioral development. *American Journal of Orthopsychiatry*, 1960, **30**, 306–314. [p. 311]

Thorpe, W. H. *Science, man and morals*. Ithaca: Cornell University Press, 1965. [p. 126]

Tietze, C. Abortion on request: Its consequences for population trends and public health. In R. B. Sloane (Ed.), *Abortion: Changing views and practice*. New York: Grune & Stratton, 1970.

Tinbergen, N. *The study of instinct*. London: Oxford University Press, 1951.

Tizard, J., & Tizard, B. The social development of two-year-old children in residential nurseries, ERIC Document PS004 892 (1967).

Turner, C. D. *General endocrinology*. (3rd ed.) Philadelphia: Saunders, 1960. [p. 435]

Tylor, E. On a method of investigating the development of institutions, applied to laws of marriage and descent. *Journal of the Royal Anthropological Institute*, 1889, **18**, 245–272.

Tyson, R. M. A 15-year study of prematurity from the standpoint of incidence, mortality, and survival. *Journal of Pediatrics*, 1946, **28**, 648–664.

United Nations. *Yearbook of the United Nations*. [vol. 3] New York: United Nations Publications: 1949.

U. S. Department of Health, Education, and Welfare. Interval between first marriage and legitimate first birth, United States, 1964–66. *Monthly Vital Statistics Report, Supplement*, 1970, **18** (12), 1–4.

U. S. House of Representatives. Effects of population growth on natural resources and the environment. Hearings before a subcommittee of the Committee on Government Operations [the Reuss Committee]. 91st Congress, 1st session, 15–16 September, 1969, pp. 74–86.

van de Velde, T. *Sex hostility in marriage*. Translated by H. Marr. London: William Heinemann, 1931. [pp. 70, 76, 78]

Waal, N. A special technique of psychotherapy with an autistic child. In G. Caplan (Ed.), *Emotional problems of early childhood*. New York: Basic Books, 1955.

Waetjen, W. B., & Grambs, J. D. Sex differences: A case of educational evasion? *Teachers College Record*, 1963, **65**, 261–271.

Wainwright, W. H. Fatherhood as a precipitant of mental illness. *American Journal of Psychiatry*, 1966, **123**, 40–44.

Waller, W. & Hill, R. *The family—a dynamic interpretation*. New York: Dryden, 1951.

Walters, R. H., & Parke, R. D. The role of the distance receptors in the development of social responsiveness. In L. P. Lipsitt & C. C. Spiker (Eds.), *Advances in child development and behavior*. Vol. 2. New York: Academic Press, 1965.

Watson, G. Happiness among adult students of education. *Journal of Educational Psychology*, 1930, **21**, 79–109.

Weidemann, J. Das Kind im Heim. *Zeitschrift für Kinderpsychiatrie*, 1959, **26**, 1–10.

Westermarck, E. *A short history of marriage*. London: Macmillan, 1926. [pp. 241, 2, 20, 254, 301]

———. *The future of marriage in western civilisation*. New York: Macmillan, 1936.

White, B. L. Child development research: An edifice without a foundation. *Merrill-Palmer Quarterly*, 1969, **15**, 49–79.

White, B. L., & Held, R. Plasticity of sensorimotor development. In J. F. Rosenblith & W. Allinsmith (Eds.), *The causes of behavior: Readings in child development and educational psychology*. (2nd ed.) Boston: Allyn & Bacon, 1966.

Whiting, J. W., Kluckhohn, R., & Anthony, A. The function of male initiation ceremonies at puberty. In E. E. Maccoby, T. M. Newcomb, & E. L. Hartley (Eds.), *Readings in social psychology*. (3rd ed.) New York: Holt, 1958.

Whitman, C. O. The behavior of pigeons. *Publications of Carnegie Institution of Washington*, 1919, **257** (3), 1–161. Cited by O. Riddle, Prolactin or progesterone as key to parental behaviour: A review.*Animal Behaviour*, 1963, **11**, 419–432.

Whitten, C. F., Pettit, M. G., & Fischhoff, J. Evidence that growth failure from maternal deprivation is secondary to undereating. *Journal of the American Medical Association*, 1969, **209**, 1675–1682.

Whyte, W. H., Jr. *The organization man*. New York: Simon & Schuster, 1956.

Wilcox, D. A. A study of three hundred and thirty premature infants.*American Journal of Diseases of Children*, 1936, **52**, 848–862.

Wilson, P. D., & Riesen, A. H. Visual development in rhesus monkeys neonatally deprived of patterned light. *Journal of Comparative and Physiological Psychology*, 1966, **61**, 87–95.

Winch, R. F. The study of personality in the family setting. *Social Forces*, 1950, **28**, 310–316.

Winch, R. F., Ktsanes, T., & Ktsanes, V. The theory of complementary needs in mate-selection: An analytic and descriptive study.*American Sociological Review*, 1954, **19**, 241–249.

Windle, W. F. Brain damage by asphyxia at birth. *Scientific American*, 1969, **221** (4), 76–84.

Wittels, F. Sadistic tendencies in parents. In V. F. Calverton & S. D. Schmalhausen (Eds.), *The new generation*. New York: Macaulay, 1930.

Wolins, M. Young children in institutions: Some additional evidence.*Developmental Psychology*, 1970, **2**, 99–109.

Woolley, C. L. *The Sumerians*. Oxford: Clarendon Press, 1928. [pp. 102, 103–104]

Wootton, B. *Social science and social pathology*. London: George Allen & Unwin, 1959.

Wortis, H. Discussion. *American Journal of Orthopsychiatry*, 1960, **30**, 547–552.

Wunderlich, R. C. Hypokinetic disease. *Academic Therapy Quarterly*, 1967, **2**, 183–189.

Wylie, P. *Generation of vipers*. New York: Rinehart, 1946.

Yarrow, L. J. Research in dimensions of early maternal care. *Merrill-Palmer Quarterly*, 1963, **9**, 101–114.

Zimmerman, C. C. *Family and civilization*. New York: Harper, 1947. [pp. 150, 14, 297]

Zitrin, A., Ferber, P., & Cohen, D. Pre- and paranatal factors in mental disorders of children. *Journal of Nervous and Mental Disease*, 1964, **139**, 357–361.

Zubek, J. P., Flye, J., & Aftanas, M. Cutaneous sensitivity after prolonged visual deprivation. *Science*, 1964, **144**, 1591–1593.

Author Index

Adams, J. T., 52
Adams, S. H., 125
Aftanas, M., 109
Alpert, A., 85, 115
Anderson, J. E., 87
Angermeier, W. F., 198
Anthony, A., 136
Aquinas, T., 49
Aristotle, 110
Ashley Montagu, M. F., *see* Montagu
Askew, M. W., 34
Aubry, J., 197
Augustine, Saint, 49, 191

Babcock, C. G., 84, 195
Baber, R. E., 43, 51, 52, 61, 185
Bacon, F., 143
Baker, R., 207
Bakwin, H., 83, 85–86, 96
Bakwin, R., 96
Bales, R. F., 38, 186, 202
Balint, M., 38
Banham, K. M., 89
Barber, E., 119
Barnes, A. C., 119, 139, 142
Bartlett, G. A., 19, 188
Bass, L. G., 81
Baumrind, D., 112
Bayley, N., 89
Beck, E. C., 199
Becker, H., 133
Beckett, P. G., 94
Bell, R. R., 200
Bender, L., 95
Berger, P. L., 53
Bergler, E., 192, 193
Berkson, J., 141
Bernard, J., 124
Bertoye, P., 197

Beskow, B., 82
Bexton, W. H., 98
Beyle, M. H. [Stendhal], 186
Bierce, A., 201–202
Bindra, D., 107, 112
Birdwhistell, R. I., 190
Blake, J., 161
Blood, R. O., 192, 206
Bodman, F., 80
Boffey, P. M., 194
Boll, E. S., 121
Booth, M., 202
Borgatta, M. L., 192
Bossard, J., 121
Bovard, E. W., Jr., 109
Bowlby, J., 85–86, 88, 115, 194, 195
Brackbill, Y., 198
Brennemann, J., 197
Bressler, B., 103
Bridges, K., 196
Briffault, R., 3, 5, 8, 14, 15, 18, 19, 46, 49, 72, 73, 187, 189, 202
Broderick, C. B., 40
Brody, S., 101, 196
Broom, L., 135
Brown, S., 118, 200
Bühler, K., 196
Burgess, E. W., 190, 201
Burlingham, D., 86

Cadwallader, M., 40, 125, 144, 151
Cairns, R. B., 107
Caldwell, B. M., 163
Calverton, V. F., 131, 135, 143, 190, 209
Cantarow, E., 127, 177
Carr, J. E., 203
Casler, L., 51, 77, 85, 88, 91, 92, 93–94, 100, 190, 193, 195,

Subject Index

Abolition of marriage, 55, 177–178
Abortion, 66, 67–68
Academic achievement, effects of parental affection, 135
Adoption, 73, 81, 150, 194
Adultery, 5, 24, 47, 120, 149–150
Age, 12, 30, 121, 153
   of separation from mother, 79–80, 85, 87, 100–101, 194
   and sexual behavior, 166, 200–201
Aggressiveness, 95
Anaclitic depression, 87
Ancestor worship, 12, 21
Animals, infra-human (*see also* specific animals)
   effects of maternal deprivation, 105–107
   mating patterns in, 2–3, 185
   parental drives, 65, 66, 70, 194
   effects of perceptual deprivation, 94, 96, 99, 104–105, 198
Annulment, 41, 120
Anthropology; *see* Cross-cultural research
Anxiety, 103, 135–136
Army of Industry, 207
Asphyxia, 195
Auditory stimulation; *see* Stimulation
Australia, infanticide in, 71
Autism, 82, 196

Baby sitters, 30
"Belongingness," need for, 20
Birth rate; *see* Population
Brain, 108, 195

Breast feeding, 11, 42, 71–72, 83–84, 194, 195
"Bruce effect," 4

Caribbean countries, illegitimacy in, 25
Catholicism, 46, 48, 119
Cattell Infant Scale, 97
Chastity, 43, 47, 49, 191
Child abuse, 133, 163, 203
Child-free marriage, 150, 171, 205
Child-bearing and -rearing (*see also* Fatherhood; Instincts; Institutions, Child-care; Legitimacy; Mothering; Parental care; Post-partum disturbances; Social pressure)
   in communes, 156, 162
   effects on parents, 127–130
   function of marriage, 10–12, 31–32, 53, 75, 116, 209
   motives for, 59–75, 127, 129, 193, 200
   in other societies, 112–115, 198, 206
   in permissive matrimony, 150, 153, 155, 158–163, 171–172
   social pressures against, 193
Children
   economic value of, 7, 12, 60–61, 128–129
   effect on marriage, 119, 122, 128, 150, 202
   unwanted, 42, 69, 80, 82, 159
Chimpanzees, 96, 104, 106
China, parent-child separation in, 113
Christianity (*see also* Catholicism, Church of England, Council of Trent, Protestant